Words of praise for *LifePath*

"Like a lathe , a journal forces us inward to the heart of the wood, a particularly necessary occupation in an age devoted to surfaces. Luci Shaw's book should lead even the most timorous and inexperienced chronicler gently into the wide expanses of inner space."

Virginia Stem Owens,
author of *Feast of Families*

"*Life Path* provides a window for a life that is more creative, thoughtful, and joyful. I found it a treasure."

Howard Hovde,
Director of Laity Lodge

"During a decade of leading journal workshops, I have wanted to recommend a book on journal keeping written by a mature Christian. At last, Luci Shaw's *Life Path*, with its poignant self-disclosure and thoughtful exercises, meets that need."

Virginia Hearn,
Adjunct Professor of
Communications, New College Berkley

" In her previous books, Luci Shaw has been adept at linking her words with her life. In *Life Path* she tells us how to combine our own."

Margaret Smith,
author of the forthcoming book,
Journal Keeper

Life Path

Personal and Spiritual Growth through Journal Writing

Luci Shaw

MULTNOMAH

Portland, Oregon

Cover design by Durand Demlow

LIFE PATH
© 1991 by Luci Shaw
Published by Multnomah Press
10209 SE Division Street
Portland, Oregon 97266

Multnomah Press is a ministry of Multnomah School of the Bible, 8435 NE Glisan Street, Portland, Oregon 97220.

Printed in the United States of America.

Library of Congress Cataloging-in-Publication Data
  Shaw, Luci.
  Life path : personal and spiritual growth through journal writing / Luci Shaw.
     p.   cm.
  On t.p. hyphen appears as an asterisk.
  Includes bibliographical references.
  ISBN 0-88070-459-4
  1. Spiritual life. 2. Diaries—Authorship—Religious aspects—Christianity. I.
  Title.
  BV4509.5.S44   1991
  158'.1—dc20   91-21878
                                                                       CIP

91 92 93 94 95 96 97 98 99 - 10 9 8 7 6 5 4 3 2 1

for Madeleine and Margaret:
exemplars in the art
of journal keeping

Contents

Foreword

Life Path will be a delight equally to inveterate journal keepers like me, and to those who've often thought they might like to keep a journal but haven't quite known how to go about it, or been timid at the prospect.

In *Life Path* Luci Shaw gives us permission—permission to keep our journals in any way that is best for us. For the new journaler (which, as she points out, is very different from journalist) she provides many helpful suggestions, starting with good advice on the kind of physical journal that will best meet our needs.

I like to buy a journal each time I take a major trip, as a reminder of the places I've been and the people I've met. Each journal thus has a history before I begin to fill the first page. The journal I bought last year in Japan has its pages marked off in squares for the Japanese characters. It was fun to fill it with my own western writing. I started it on a futon on a tatami mat in Tokyo, and finished it in my apartment in New York. I've just come to the last page of an enormous and beautiful journal bought in New Valomo in Finland as I began a trip to Russia. It was heavy to travel with despite its beauty, so it is with relief that I have started a much smaller journal the day before setting off from northwest Connecticut to Chicago and Wheaton College, a journal given me by the owner of a delightful bookstore where I'd spent several hours autographing.

Indeed, as Luci Shaw points out, anything goes. The point is to write, to fill the journals with thoughts, prayers, hopes, griefs, yes, and angers and disappointments, too. The journal is ours. Our own unique story between us and God, and God knows all our emotions, including those we may have been taught to repress.

In writing a journal as honestly as a human being can write, we are given the opportunity to write our own story, to have a say in the direction our lives are going. It is wondrous how writing something out helps us to see it in an objective way that wouldn't be possible otherwise. Luci Shaw provides suggestions, questions, delightful quotations by other journal writers.

I agree with her that a journal is best written as a whole, not divided into a spiritual journal, a journal of events, or any other separation of sacred and secular. The Word that created a universe indeed created a *uni*verse, and the Incarnation emphasizes that all is sacred. No matter how much we may try to secularize, we never quite succeed. Even if we are writing about preparing for a dinner party, we are still writing a spiritual journal, for surely hospitality is part of our spirituality. So is setting down the wondrous words of our children (or grandchildren) which we will forget unless we write them down.

No thing is inappropriate for a journal. God can take our grumpiness, our anger, our fear; and our fumbling words can suddenly be given new meaning and we glimpse a new understanding of redemption. Yes, in *Life Path* Luci Shaw gives practical hints for journal keeping which can be invaluable to the beginning journaler. But even more valuable than that is the freedom she offers to keep our journals in whatever way suits us best.

Madeleine L'Engle

Chapter 1

The Power of
Journal Writing

All kinds of words could be used to describe what keeping a reflective journal will do for the one who writes it; writing a journal regularly will enrich, nourish, mature, heal, develop, broaden, enhance, and transform you. No doubt about it, if you become a consistent journal keeper, you will change, and be changed.

I could list numbers of well-known journal writers and the titles of their published journals to demonstrate this, among them Augustine's *Confessions*, *The Diary of a Young Girl* by Anne Frank, the journals of Lewis and Clark, *The Life and Diary of David Brainerd*, Blaise Pascal's *Pensees*, Anne Morrow Lindburgh's series of published journals and many others. But maybe two case-histories will serve as examples:

Sharon Earl, a young married woman who spent a week with me in a journal workshop last summer, wrote to me:

The first assignment you gave us, "to write, concretely and honestly, about a relationship," had enormous impact for me. I decided to write about my sister who died in May. I felt I had dealt with my grief and did not feel particularly emotional as I began to write. I ended up writing my memories of her since her birth (she was four years younger than I).

As I journaled (and journeyed) through her life I was shocked at the well of grief that gushed through me. I spent a good amount of time in deep, primal sobbing. I began to see patterns in my relationship to her that I hadn't noticed before, and areas of hurt that I'd been afraid to look at.

In my journal process I let myself consciously feel the lack of sister-closeness that pervaded our childhood. As her big sister, I often ignored her, occupied as I was with growing up and being with my own friends. Our four-year gap meant that when she was in high school, I was in college. When she was in college, I married. Our lives didn't really begin to cross until we both became mothers.

Soon after I became a mother, my husband and I left for Kenya with our child, as missionaries. A month after our arrival, my husband died in an auto accident. For the next year, I was grieving, single-mothering, and healing. I also began dating my second husband, Shep. After we married, I became pregnant again when, BAM!, the news of my sister's diagnosis—acute myloblastic leukemia—hit me like a blow in the gut. I desperately wanted to be close to her, care for her, be there, make up for lost time, and claim the sisterhood that we should have had. Slowly God began to redeem our relationship in those final days, though my pain distanced me at times. I gave her a mug that said, "My Sister, My Friend," and meant it with all my heart. Later Mom told me that my sister had said, "That mug that

Sharon gave me—the sister mug—I wish I could take it to heaven."

But it was through this process of journaling that God became more real for me, and I experienced his healing and forgiveness.

In *The Genesse Diary*, Henri Nouwen, the well-known writer and speaker, tells of his experience during a seven-month stay in a Trappist monastery. As he participated in the daily routines of work and prayer at the Abbey of the Genesee in upstate New York, he kept a journal that reflects all his conflicting desires and questions, his moments of misgiving as well as his joy, and a new sense of integration and expectation, which seems to have come as much from keeping the journal as from the monastic experience itself. Because it was a private journal, never intended for publication, the result was a book of penetrating honesty, no holds barred. I recommend it as a superb model for journal writing. As you read it you can feel Nouwen's growth in self-knowledge and God-knowledge; he was being changed as he wrote.

Here's what Nouwen says about writing in *The Genesee Diary*:

It is a remarkable sensation to see ideas and words flowing so easily, as if they had always been there, waiting.

Meanwhile, I am becoming more and more aware that for me writing is a very powerful way of concentrating and of clarifying for myself many thoughts and feelings. Once I put pen on paper and write for an hour or two, a real sense of peace and harmony comes to me. . . . After a day without any writing . . . I often have a general feeling of mental constipation and go to bed with the sense that I did not do what I should have done that day.

Here we have examples of the power of journal writing

in two very different contexts, from two different writers. One a woman, one a man. One a young homemaker, one an experienced and prominent spiritual leader and writer.

As you read this book and put its ideas into action, realize that you fit somewhere between these two. You don't need to be an expert, you just need to have the desire and discipline to do it.

Just Do It

Though I have read a number of books about journal keeping, since I began to teach it and write about it, I began quite simply, without any formal instruction, by just doing it as a means of holding onto my sanity during a time of profound personal crisis.

I learned as I went along. That is the method I recommend to you. So, think of me not as an expert but as an ordinary person sharing what I have learned by trial and error. In these chapters I'll do what I do when I teach the writing of poetry: I'll say to you, "This worked for me; try it yourself."

Maybe you can think of me as the midwife who helps you deliver the thoughts and insights waiting inside you to be born, assisting in their birth. Or the coach in your Lamaze experience. In that role I can suggest some practicalities, give some examples from my own journals and those of others, recommend some techniques and exercises to get you going, and stimulate your thinking and your imagination.

I cannot live your life, nor conceive ideas for you, nor cultivate their growth into words. That is a cooperative effort between you and God, and it takes time, just as the gestation of a human baby takes time. Your seminal experience with God, your personal and spiritual growth will be yours alone.

I can share experiences that are common enough for us all to participate in. I hope I can demonstrate that in the most ordinary events and thoughts God is at work, walking beside us on our journey, showing us its meaning, if we are willing to listen, and to see.

While keeping track of that for myself, I'd like to share with you how, by reflective journal keeping, you can chart the path of your life, seeing patterns, themes, and metaphors that provide you with perspective.

Life Path has been designed with wide margins so you can make your own notes and comments as you go along. On these margins you will also find cogent quotations, all from writers of journals. You may ask, "Who are these people?" Many of them are private individuals who have participated in my journal workshops, and have given me permission to use their observations. Other quotes come from well-known authors or teachers, or from personal friends.

Throughout the pages of this book I have suggested exercises in which you can experiment with different aspects of journal writing. (You may wish to use the companion "blank book" designed to my suggested specifications, available from Multnomah Press.) The exercises will give you simple but basic experience in using journal techniques. Although these exercises are optional I recommend them as ways you can demonstrate to yourself that writing is not only possible for you; it is fun, and it is worthwhile. What you discover for yourself by experience is nearly always a better motivator than hearing what someone else has discovered.

Just as Sharon Earl's journal became, among other things, a catalyst for her own emotional healing and growth, just as Henri Nouwen's journal writing made him aware of the creative process that begins with putting pen to paper (and his writing, not incidentally, is helping to shape the thinking of our generation), so your own writing of a journal will change and teach you, and perhaps allow your writing skills to develop enough to effect changes in others who read your writing.

So, what are you waiting for? Begin.

Chapter 2

Getting Going:
Tools for Journal Writing

What Tools Do I Need, and How Do I Use Them?

After building my cabin in the woods in Washington, one of my first urgent desires was to tame the wilderness that surrounded the small, solar home. This meant subduing the chaos of blackberries, eliminating the riot of weeds, and planning a setting of rustic beauty and order. In my old jeans and boots I sallied forth to attack the space between house and stream.

I soon realized that something was missing. For starters, I needed garden gloves and clippers, a hack saw for errant branches, and a wheelbarrow to cart away debris to the burn pile. Before the job was finished, I had made trips without number to the gardening section of Fred Meyer's for other basic equipment—rakes, shovels, a trowel, peat moss, snailbait, hose and watering can, seeds, seedlings, fertilizer . . . and some trips to the Nooksack River to harvest the wonderful water-smooth stones that anchor my rock garden today.

There are very few activities that don't need some specific basic equipment. Whether you're gardening, snorkeling, dress-making, skiing, cooking, or taking photographs, you need the appropriate gear. Fortunately, the tools for journal keeping are few and simple: basically, you need something to write *on*, and something to write *with*. If your motivation is very high—"I just *have to journal* or I'll die, go crazy, shrivel up inside . . ."—you can get by with almost any writing surface and implement. Most of us, though, need to choose our tools with care, because they subtly shape the ease with which we write, what we write, and the way we write it.

Choosing a Journal

Do you constantly write ideas and quotes you want to remember on the backs of envelopes? Do you jot descriptive phrases on your current shopping list? Then you are the kind of person for whom choosing an appropriate journal makes sense. To give your writing the importance it deserves, rather than keep your scribbled-on paper scraps in a box (some people actually do this) you need clean, white space bound into the safety, and permanence, of a journal.

There's a wide range of "blank books" to choose from— a cheap pad of paper (which will fall apart, and which shows what you *really* think about yourself keeping a journal), and a journal so beautiful and expensive that it discourages trivialities (which are the things that make up most of life anyway).

Between these extremes you must find, as Tristine Rainer suggests in *The New Diary*, the "balance between respect for yourself, represented by your involvement in the diary process, and a consideration of the freedom you need to feel that you can do anything you wish on the pages."

First of all, the kind of notebook or journal you write in (size, binding, lined or blank pages) will affect the way you write.

If you use a small notebook it may cramp not only your hand-writing but your style. But it has the advantage of convenience. You can easily slip it in your purse or pocket. It works for the details in the cracks of your life.

If you use a large journal, 8½-by-11-inch paper, for instance, the very size of the blank page may at first be intimidating (all that white space to fill). But it's easier to rest your hand on, and you may come to relish the space and freedom of the larger page. It may even enlarge your thinking.

Because this large format notebook is usually hole-punched, when you have filled it you can bind it in a three-ring binder and store it on a bookshelf. Resist the impulse, though, to use the three-ring binder itself as a journal. Sure, you can add and subtract pages at will, but it may also make you think of schoolwork and you could become preoccupied with filing, arranging, categorizing and rewriting your entries in a way that destroys the spontaneous "stream of life" process that seems to be most productive for journal keepers.

If you use one of the beautiful leather or cloth-covered journals on heavy, creamy paper without ruled lines (once you become known as a journal keeper, kind friends will gift-wrap them for your birthday without fail) you may be frustrated that it doesn't lie flat, or stay open easily. And you can't tear pages out of it as readily. But it will hold your precious confidences in safety, and by its appearance and cost it will represent how important your journal is to you.

One good choice is a spiral-bound, 9½-by-6-inch ruled notebook (if you like to sketch or illustrate your journal, find one without lines). You can buy these with plastic or cardboard covers. The plastic holds up under brutal treatment; the cardboard looks and feels better. This notebook opens easily, and stays open *flat*. You can clip your pen in place within its metal spiral. And when it's full, it stacks

A small notebook can be kept in your pocket, but then you will have small thoughts. That's OK. William Carlos Williams, the great American poet who was also a children's doctor, wrote many of his poems on prescription pads.
—Natalie Goldberg
Writing Down the Bones

My journal is about 8-by-4 inches. I have it with me always. If I'm waiting in lines at the grocery story, I can always open my purse and pull it out. A lot of my entries begin "Safeway."
—Karen Rosenbaum, writing teacher

The pen you write with . . . should be a fast-writing pen because your thoughts are always much faster than your hand. You don't want to slow your hand even more with a slow pen.
—Natalie Goldberg
Writing Down the Bones

well in a bookcase along with other books, unlike a larger-size notebook that sticks out from the shelf.

What to Write With

What about your writing implement? The ink in some felt tips and pens bleeds through paper. Check that the combination of pen and paper you are using results in a clear, clean impression, and doesn't show through to the other side when you turn the page. Some writers enjoy using a pencil, especially if they are perfectionists; it allows them to erase and correct. Others prefer a good ball-point pen.

Using different colored inks for different kinds of writing, as some do, presupposes an organized mind belonging to a writer who has the right colors available at all times.

If you're like me, you use whatever's handy because you don't want to lose a thought while searching your house for the right pen or pencil. If you're organized, you can attach that perfect writing tool to your journal and keep it for that task alone; no borrowing it for other tasks in critical moments.

Handwriting is more adaptable to varied circumstances than typewriting or word-processing. And hand-writing is uniquely you—your body communicating directly with your journal pages so that even the feel of your hand-heel resting on the paper becomes part of a familiar, well-loved process. Novelist Graham Greene observed, "Some authors type their works, but I cannot do that. Writing is tied up with the hand, almost with a special nerve." For journal keeping, the most intensely personal kind of writing, this seems especially true.

Signposts along the Path

Write your name, address and phone number on the journal's cover (or fly leaf) so that if lost, it can be returned to you. (Later, I'll tell the story of how miraculously this worked for me.) Your journal will become important to you, as mine has to me. If our house caught fire, my instinctive reaction would be to rescue my journals and photographs before anything else.

Also on the cover, under your name, write the beginning date (and the ending date when the journal is full), and number each volume in sequence.

Number each page, for easier referral back to things you want to remember. If an entry is especially important, use a highlighting pen to help you find it again.

Date each entry (not just "Monday morning," but "Monday morning, March 16"). Dates are the mileposts along your life-path.

Your Best Friend: An Available Journal

Why all the emphasis on keeping your journal handy? *Because you can never predict what a day will bring. Or when you will need it.* Almost without exception. I regret it if I decide to leave my journal at home. Some crucial mental or spiritual transaction, which needs to be described while it's fresh, will occur. Or a poem starts in my mind . . . and I have to write it in on a deposit slip in my checkbook. Who knows when that important decision will come clear to you, or you'll see or hear something that makes everything "click into place"? If you don't write it down right away, even in the middle of the night, it may evaporate by the time you and your journal are reunited.

Sometimes driving to my office I'll receive the first line of a poem. Or in the night I'll think of the lead-in for an article, or a way to handle a problem relationship. Or listening to the sermon in church on Sunday I'll hear something so significant for me, some connection or image I haven't noticed before, that I know I mustn't lose it.

And there, beside me on the seat of the car, or in my purse or briefcase, or on my bedside table, or on the pew

I put a piece of paper
under my pillow, and
when I could not sleep
I wrote in the dark.
—Henry David
Thoreau, naturalist

beside me, is my friend the journal, ready, as always, to receive whatever I have to give it.

In my poem "First Draft" I describe how I have to seize poetic ideas gently yet firmly in the dark of night, without turning on the light or having to search for a pencil.

> When you hear them
> coming through
> the blank air,
> you must slap them down,
> like mosquitoes, or they'll
> vanish behind the
> furniture.

(Solution: I keep my journal and pen within reach on my night table.) Anything that takes time or distracts me may bleach away the image, dilute the idea, or banish it completely, like a dream that is sucked away in the moment of waking.)

The poem ends like this:

> If you are brave,
> so that they have confidence
> in you, the lines
> will be there
> when you wake, telling
> your vision back to you.

Rereading your journal, and knowing that your words have captured your idea perfectly and permanently, brings a special kind of satisfaction. Kathy Penner, one of my journal workshop members, expresses it perfectly: "Things flit through my head that I know God has put there, but I'm too busy to pay much attention. Writing makes me listen. Somehow putting it down in blue and white makes it more real. I guess we're concrete, physical people. Thoughts, revelations, epiphanies, float away and are lost in the crowd of happenings. I tie these things down, own them, when I write."

One note set down on
the spot is worth a
whole carload of later
reminiscences.
—Thomas Gray,
poet

Shifting the Weight from Mind to Paper

My journal gives me a way to relieve the burden of excitement or revelation.

Sometimes I get so full of ideas (especially on my morning walk) that the fear of losing them creates its own kind of anxiety. That's why I nearly always carry my journal with me and jot down things as they happen or thoughts as they occur to me.

This was quite a trick when I was traveling on a safari van in a game reserve in Africa, with rutted dirt tracks and red dust swirling. Every few seconds I had to leap to my feet and photograph a zebra or a giraffe. I'm a knitter and a photographer as well as a writer, and keeping all three activities going at once in a bumpy van required some fancy finger-work. All my friends on the trip grew intensely interested in my journal, often trying to read over my shoulder to see if I'd said anything about *them* or quoted their cogent remarks.

Journal Options for the Technology Buff

1. The tape recorder. I made a passing reference to this earlier. There are some appealing hand-held recorders available now, and some people find it quicker and easier to tape than to write, especially when driving. But unless you transcribe your spoken thoughts into your written journal right away, you will have trouble finding specific journal entries later, when you want them.

2. The typewriter or the personal computer. This makes for speedy writing and readable copy. But even the lightest lap-top is more cumbersome to carry than a notebook. Such hi-tech methods may seem less personal, too mechanical for some. And with a PC there are always the problems of portability or availability, as well as of power-source or replacing batteries.

Decision-time.

There's nothing to writing. All you do is sit down and open a vein.
—Rod Smith, author

You may go for looks, or you may go for practicality, but whatever you do, you must find what works best, and is most comfortable and convenient for you. As a first step, turn theory into practice, and . . .

Try this:

Go to your local stationer's or gift shop, and examine all the notebooks and pens available, for looks, for feel, for convenience, for expense. Then take your pick and purchase a journal (don't forget to check if your journal of choice lies flat when you open it) and an appropriate pen.

Make this decision carefully. You may be living with it for a while.

1. In the space below (or in your journal) write "Time Clock." Draw the face of a clock *without hands* but fill in the numbers.

2. As you look at the clock you have drawn, ask "What time is it in my life?" Let the question sink in until you feel as though the right time has suggested itself to you. Draw two hands on the clock face to represent the time.

3. Write one or two descriptive sentences that would address the question: Where am I in my life right now?" Such as:

> I feel as if my life is standing still. . . .
> I'm in a lonely, lost time. . . .
> This is a time of new beginnings. . . .

4. Meditate for a minute on what it means to you to be in this time in your life. Allow circumstances or feelings that affect this time to come to the surface. Write down what you are thinking.

5. What brought you to this time in your life? Is there any significant event or change that seems to mark this period?

6. What *color* best describes this time for you?

7. What *sounds* do you hear?

8. What *adjectives* best describe your life right now?

9. What *feelings* dominate you?

10. What *people* or *events* affect your life significantly?

11. How long has this period lasted?

12. Take time to talk this out with yourself and God, telling what you've discovered about yourself today. Pray, listening for what God is telling you in your heart.

Chapter 3

Journaling
and Journeying

It was 3:00 in the afternoon. Through the Venetian blinds of the surgeon's office in the hospital the sunlight filtered in in narrow strips. The sharp images of light and shadow are still burned into my memory.

I had spent the morning in the waiting room next to the Intensive Care Unit in our local hospital. In the ICU lay my husband, Harold, following surgery, attached to an array of intimidating hardware—monitors and tubes and gauges. The room was never still; nurses and technicians moved in and out, endlessly checking.

Harold lay there, unconscious of this seeming confusion. He was out of it. Literally. And with machines breathing for him and keeping track of his pulse and brain activity, I felt like an unnecessary onlooker. Heavily-sedated, semi-conscious, he was barely aware of my presence.

At noon I had been summoned to the surgeon's office. Casually the great man sat on the edge of his desk and gestured for me to sit down. In a clinical, unemotional voice he said, "Harold has adenocarcinoma of the lung (cancer). We have removed his lung, but he probably has less than eighteen months to live."

In my journal I later described what at that moment felt indescribable:

> With [the surgeon's] words, clear and colorless, hang-ing in the air, I felt no sorrow or grief, just an awful numbness. I couldn't cry. I remember that in a terrible effort to move toward normalcy, like rising from an underwater dive to the surface of a lake, I asked him some questions. My legs felt heavy, as if I'd been drugged.

> That was the day when the fabric of our lives was ripped down the middle. Though we were surrounded by supportive friends, though some of our children were with us, and the others I could reach by phone to unload my feelings, I was cut off from the one closest to me, with whom I had shared the secrets of my heart, my questions, my fears, my moments of vision and despair and joy.

In this new crisis I felt the urgent need for an outlet for expression, some way of keeping not just a record of the *events*—dramatic, radical, critical as they were—but a way of verbalizing *how I felt about what was happening*, what my medical and spiritual questions were, what I was praying, how my emotional weather fluctuated in the pressure sys-tems of anxiety, the warm relief I felt at a hint of good news, the shaky uncertainty that accompanied each new earthquake that was heaving up our orderly, productive lives.

I call it *the crucible effect*; when the heat is on, things either melt or harden, depending on whether they are trivial or crucial. Issues sometimes seem to be clarified by extreme stress, showing themselves more cleanly and strongly when we look them in the face. Cancer does that for you.

So does war. Or persecution. Or divorce. Or death. You realize what is vital in life, and, by contrast, what is absolutely not worth spending worry on.

But to retain the significance of the events I learned I had to *write them down* and reflect on them. I didn't want all that I was living and learning to be lost in the blur of those crowded, emotion-filled days. I wanted to remember because I sensed the importance of those transitions.

That was when, that was why, I became a journal writer.

In my journal I wrote: "I want to catch and preserve the pain of these days—learning about life with cancer. The hours won't linger to be experienced again, but they are valuable, precious. All I can hope is that these words in my journal . . . will summon up enough detail to recall some of each hour's immediate reality."

Journaling and Journeying

Each of our lives is a journey, with a beginning (the past), and an end (somewhere in the future), with the present sandwiched in between—where we are, and the steps we are taking now. A journal helps us to follow and chart our life paths, logging our progress in much the same way as the skipper of a ship writes into the log at the end of a day the distance traveled, the weather conditions, any difficulties encountered, anything unusual, and the position of the ship—an X on the chart, showing its latitude and longitude.

There is a clear connection between *journal keeping* and *journeying*. Each speaks of the progress made in a day (the French word *jour* means *day*.) Journal keeping is a record of your spiritual, emotional, intellectual, or artistic traveling, your personal edging closer to God, reality, true perception, and self-knowledge.

If you were to hike the Appalachian Trail, you wouldn't expect to cover the two thousand miles from Maine to Georgia in a few days. If you had some magic method of

"Jules Weiss suggests that one sees life as a journey starting from where we are to who we truly are: 'Writing encourages discovery of where I am, who I am, what I'm going through, and enables me to use the present moment as an opportunity for growth.'"
—Esther Jarratt, teacher

speeding along a foot trail at one hundred miles an hour you would reach the goal sooner but you would miss the whole point of the hike, which is to *walk* your way along the top of one of the most lovely mountain ranges in the United States.

Each day your progress would be significant not only in terms of the miles you covered, but in your experience of breathtaking views—dust-blue peaks, mist-filled valleys, the quiet stillness of early mornings, the shy animals, the incredible profusion of flowers and grasses and trees, the people you meet—fellow-travelers and local residents, your feelings of exaltation, or energy, or exhaustion, the condition of the track, the changes in weather, the slow shifting of seasons, your reactions to seeing the landscape both close up and far away, in depth and from a broader perspective.

And, of course, how your feet are holding up.

It's the small, concrete, transient details, and your response to them, as well as the wider views, that make the whole experience memorable.

The analogy applies to the keeping of a journal. Your life consists of a journey crowded with myriad details, circumstances, experiences, people. With a journal you can observe it all from your own unique perspective and keep track of it as you go, progressing in small, daily, even hourly, increments.

I was delighted to find that the word *safari* is Swahili for *journey.* Having gone on safari in Kenya, I can apply to journal writing something of the sense of anticipation, adventure, and discovery which I experienced in a setting as similar to my idea of Eden as anything I have seen.

So, a journal, or diary, is "a book of days," a report, written to yourself, which, in a curious way, gives you a sense of continuity and control over often uncontrollable events.

"I . . . write about my angers and fears and hurts, depressions and disappointments and anxieties, my joys and thanksgivings. . . . In short, I set down the feelings and events that have mattered to me, high moments and low. . . . The journal is like a little island of solid rock on which we can stand and see the waves and storms for what they really are."
—Morton Kelsey
The Other Side of Silence

Writing Your Own History

If we keep a record of our past—where we have been—it may provide us with clues about the future—where we are going. None of us wants to feel that we are "standing still." We need the sense of forward movement to give our lives meaning and purpose. A journal provides proof that a personal history is being built, and will progress. Author Ann Long, in "Journal of a Lifetime," observes, "My journal consists of fragments scattered over many pages . . . which help me begin to sense the movement, direction, and shape of my life so far."

Your journal is a process, as well as a product.

Seeing the Big Picture

So valuable to me was the daily written expression that was being wrung out of me in anguish over my husband's cancer that I want to share its benefits with you.

I wrote about everything—the multiple medical procedures, tests, physicians, nurses, diagnoses, pain, chemotherapy. I wrote about the clear, golden days of remission, each one a gift to be treasured. I wrote about my struggle for stability and my growth through psychotherapy. About our grieving together. And about the final slipping away of Harold's life—how it happened, what it felt like, what I learned about death—and life. I recorded the paradoxes of faith through which I labored. I described the numbness and emotional paralysis that follows bereavement, and the slow healing of the wound.

I also included the moments of hilarity, the poems that came, like babies, with no regard for my schedule. (Poetry, like childbirth, is irresistible; once you go into labor you have to keep going through to delivery.) I wrote the details of my forward movement as life took on new meaning for me, and I began to heal and grow and flourish.

It's a story that moved in and out of shadow, between eclipse and epiphany. The result of those journals is *God in*

"I never travel without my diary. One should always have something sensational to read on the train."
—Oscar Wilde
The Importance of Being Earnest

"My poetry is, or should be, useful to me for one reason: it is the record of my individual struggle from darkness toward some measure of light."
—Dylan Thomas
in response to a 1934 questionnaire

"Why do I like to journal? Because I can 'see' the patterns more clearly when I go back months later over a chunk of my life. What was full of confusion and question now 'makes sense' and there is meaning and validation."
—Janet Taylor, counselor

the Dark, a book I wrote day by day, *as a journal*, with no thought that it would ever be published, with which many readers have identified because of the parallels in their own lives.

Now, as I reread my own account of those years I see the larger framework in which my life was being shaped; how God was at work, though at the time I often failed to recognize the cycles and patterns of his involvement with me. Reading those journals again has been enormously helpful to me.

Rereading a journal is like viewing a forest from a helicopter. From that fluid height you can see the larger contours of the land, the way the trees clump and break, the vivid color contrasts between evergreens and maples, the cliffs and streams and rocks that interrupt the flow of the landscape. When you are lost in the forests of daily crisis, caught in the underbrush, you cannot know where you are. Only from the height of passing months and years can you see your life in proportion and with true perspective.

Because of this, I urge you to set aside, at regular intervals, time to reread and digest the past as it is set down on the pages of your journal.

I have told you some of my story. Now I invite you to capture your own life in words. Though your story will be very different, as you record it in a journal you, too, will come to learn the meaning of your life.

Though you write your journal in and for the moment, it is a slice of permanent history (as long as you keep it), a chart of your path through the forest of life. When you read it over later you will find it to be a story more fascinating than a novel, a graphic travelog of your inner and outer journeyings.

Try this:

Describe some significant change-points (the *crucible effects*), either negative or positive, in your life-journey of this past year. What have you learned from them? Are you different as a result? Describe the changes. Has stress or struggle been a part of the change? If so, write about that, and about the spiritual or emotional muscles you have developed.

Chapter 4

Writing What You See

As the early sun filled the blue bowl of the harbor at Patmos, in the Greek Islands, the ship anchored and all of us who were passengers were ferried to shore. We could glimpse in the distance what we had been anticipating since the beginning of the tour—the dark, walled castle that crowns the small island of Patmos and, halfway up, the chapel that marks the site of a deep cave in the rock. This was the cave in which the aging, exiled Apostle John is said to have received his revelation from God—the Revelation which is recorded in the last book in the Bible.

Between eucalyptus and pine trees our tour group followed the upward track to the entrance of the shrine, trooped down the whitewashed steps, and crowded around the cave mouth. The grotto itself, like many holy places in the Middle East, has, sometime in the intervening centuries, become a chapel. Within it a Greek orthodox service was in progress, and we listened quietly to the chanting of the worshipers filling the rough cave, standing on its uneven rock floor with heads bowed.

It was a profoundly moving moment for me. As I stood there, with the cool shadow of the cave a deep contrast to the dazzling sunlight and whitewashed stone walls outside, I remembered the way the Apostle John's vision begins, in Revelation 1, with his vivid description of the "one like the Son of Man" (a title Jesus applied to himself). It is this radiant, heavenly figure who commands John, "with a loud voice like a trumpet . . . *Write on a scroll what you see.*" And later, after John had collapsed—overwhelmed with the glory and with fear—the command is repeated: *"Fear not; Write what you have seen"* (Revelation 1:17,19).

As a writer, I have always felt that to "write what I see" was a special command to me. A writer must be an attentive observer of whatever life-experience is granted him or her. And to be at the actual site where the original instruction was given by God reinforced its value and authority for me in an unforgettable way.

Of course, not everything we "see" today is a prophetic vision from God. But if we can shift this New Testament command into a commission for today—to write what we see—it can become a vital principle for us as journal keepers.

And, as was true for the Apostle John, one of the first essentials is to break the fear barrier.

Don't be afraid to record whatever it is that you see; write it down.

If you have never kept a journal before, or if your journal keeping has been less than successful, you may be feeling fearful, or inadequate, as many of the biblical prophets felt— even major ones like Isaiah, Jeremiah, Daniel, and John. Though we don't want to class ourselves with the prophets, like them we often feel torn in opposite directions: wanting to receive and record what we are being shown, but anxious because we're inexperienced, and we think we may not do it right. In our anxiety, we may ask questions like these:

What If I'm not a Good Writer?

Just remember, *journal keeping* and *journalism* are not synonymous terms. For you to take this "course in *Journal Keeping 101*" there are no prerequisites. You don't need a literary background. You don't have to have a professional ease with words. No editor will see, or criticize your prose. You are not writing for publication but for personal illumination, recording your own thoughts and observations for your own edification and growth. If you can write a thank-you note, or jot a memo, or scribble a shopping list, you can keep a journal.

And there are many fringe benefits. One of them is that in the process of expressing yourself on paper every day you may develop latent skills you never knew were within you, and grow a taste, and a gift for writing. In any case, you'll probably become a better writer.

Don't I Need Special Writing Techniques?

Relax. Anything goes. You can't do it wrong. In *The New Diary* Tristine Rainer suggests: "Write fast, write everything, include everything, write from your feelings, write from your body, accept whatever comes."

That's another way of saying, "Write what you see."

Sometimes in writing classes I start by asking everyone to write for ten minutes without stopping, whether or not the words seem to "make sense." This has a marvelously freeing effect. We need to be given permission to write nonsense, if that's what comes into our heads. And sometimes in the most profound way, this "nonsense" does "make sense."

Writing with freedom is like taking the cork out of a bottle so that what is inside is free to pour out. We discover what we are really thinking without having to restrain or

"When [my students] knew their work wasn't going to be corrected for spelling and composition, I discovered that I had real writers in the class. I try to turn them on to their own natural voice, and they find this very liberating. I tell them: Get in touch with who you really are and it will be a base; you will be your own best friend."
—Doret Kollerer, writing teacher

"edit" it for public consumption.

Each of us has within us what may be called an Internal Critic, or Internal Censor, who tells us our writing is idiotic, badly expressed, trivial, and that therefore we are not OK, we have nothing to say, and we're wasting our time trying to write anything, even a journal. It often helps if we can drown out that critic with the flow of our own words.

The incredible freedom of the journal is that it can be whatever you want it to be. Because it is a voluntary activity, and a private one, it can be written without most of the constraints or rules that apply to other forms of literature.

Tristine Rainer goes on to say, "There are no mistakes. At any time you can change your point of view, your style, the pen you write with, the direction you write on the pages, the language in which you write, the subjects you include. . . . You can misspell, write ungrammatically . . . curse, pray, brag, write poetically, eloquently, angrily, lovingly."

Once you've opened the dam, or have surmounted the fear barrier, and you have felt the exhilaration of writing freely, *then* you can afford to slow down and take a more meditative, thoughtful, reflective look at your life.

Try this:

Write a letter to yourself. Choose one incident, relationship, idea—something that has been burning in you, or that you are excited about. Describe it clearly, then tell yourself what you really feel about it, and why.

Or, answer these questions:

1. How was today unique, different from any other day?

2. What questions did life ask me today?

3. What did I read that caught my attention or challenged me?

4. What made me happy today? Why?

5. Did anything depress me? Why?

6. Did this day present me with a new opportunity for growth? Did I accept this opportunity? Why, or why not?

7. How do I feel about myself? My family? My friends? God?

8. Do I face any situations that need to be prayed about?

How Can I Find the Time?

Like most worthwhile efforts, writing a journal asks us to sacrifice precious time. Say you work full time at a demanding job, or have several small children. "How," you ask, "can I ever take time to consistently keep a journal?"

If you're as occupied as that, you *need* to slow down. And keeping a journal may provide that break in your busyness that will keep you sane and emotionally more healthy.

Of course, there are some shortcuts. Often during my day I will have an idea, a question, a problem, or see a connection, without having enough cracks in the schedule to write about it fully.

That's when I *make a list* of the topics I want to enlarge on later, using trigger words that will jog my memory. (Since I usually have my journal with me, I jot these list words down in pencil at the top of my current journal page.)

At the end of the day I check the list and write reflectively about my concerns. Having that list has relieved me of the fear that I may forget something really important that needs to be recorded.

When I write reflectively, my mind often races faster than my pen. I don't want to lose a thought in the rush of words and ideas, so I use my own brand of shorthand—abbreviations like "wd." for *would*, "w/" for *with*, "fr." for *from*, "b/o" for *because of*, numerals instead of written numbers, initials for the people who reappear regularly in the writing. (You'll develop your own code as you go along.)

"In a way—nobody sees a flower—really—it is so small—we haven't time—and to see takes time, like to have a friend takes time."
—Georgia O'Keeffe, painter

How Can I Guard My Private Thoughts?

The idea of writing down what you are feeling may be threatening to you. It may seem too raw, too angry, too dangerous to risk recording. And even more scary is the thought that someone else may pick up your journal and read what you have dared to write.

Total honesty is essential for the maximum benefits of journal keeping. If you gloss over problems or pains, or neglect to journal your way through them thoroughly, you will short-change yourself. Christian people in particular may hesitate to put down thoughts that seem "uncharitable" or "unchristian" to them. It's hard to be honest when you have been trained all your life to rein in or deny your strong emotions. But in working through a relationship you may need to express some difficult feelings about someone in your circle of friends or in your household. And absolute honesty requires absolute privacy.

In his book *Secrets*, Dr. Paul Tournier advances the idea that everyone, even a young child, has the right to some thoughts and ideas that are his or hers alone—that are secret, hidden from everyone. In this era of open communication, of "letting it all hang out," this may seem like heresy, but Tournier feels that having secrets, in a private part of ourselves known only to us and God, contributes to our mental health and our personal wholeness and independence.

Nevertheless, because your secret journal may be a threat, or an irresistible temptation to someone to peek, you may need to devise some safeguards to prevent indiscriminate reading of your inner thoughts.

If your family has high standards of integrity you can make a mutual pact to preserve each other's secrecy. Reinforce this by the notice, in large letters, on your journal cover: VERY PRIVATE JOURNAL, and don't leave it lying around where it can tempt the curious. Put it out of sight in a drawer, or on a high shelf. Or carry it with you.

If you have inflammatory content, and don't trust your spouse or child or roommate, lock your journal away securely.

Sometimes you may choose to share portions of what you have written with someone trustworthy like a therapist, teacher, spiritual director, pastor, or intimate friend. But remember, *that is your choice.* No one else has the right to read what you have designated as private.

Tristine Rainer points out: "Even if you never share a sentence of your diary with anyone else, you will share it through your life. Its existence will touch other people by the way it changes you and permits you to develop in self-awareness, directness, and honesty. . . . You will grow in your ability to understand and nourish others."

What If Nothing Extraordinary Happens?

A young woman came to me at a journal workshop and asked for help with a common problem. "I've tried for years to keep a journal," she said, "but it always peters out. Then, after I've let it go for a while I get discouraged—it's too difficult to catch up—and then it's hard to start again. How can I keep a journal consistently?"

One of our most nagging dilemmas is the problem of guilt, or a sense of failure, when we don't keep our commitment to write a continuing journal. Often, like this woman, we just give up. And weeks or months of our lives go unrecorded and largely forgotten until we get the next "motivation fix," and start over.

I know how tough this is. I once wrote in my journal, "Some days the ideas flow, sprouting words like green plants in the moisture of a garden in spring. Keeping a journal current is sometimes like keeping up with a fast-growing lawn; two weeks' worth of ideas and spiritual transactions, if not recorded, become as unmanageable as two weeks' worth of uncut grass."

Life is such a seasonal enterprise, with periods of

intense, unavoidable business and preoccupation. Some days seem full of interest and challenge, or satisfaction. Or relief, like the day at the doctor's office when I learned that I didn't have anything as heroic as cancer, only a rather prosaic ailment—diverticular disease—chronic, annoying, but not life-threatening.

And of course I wrote it down; *not* to have cancer was clearly an answer to prayer. But the more I wrote the more I realized that I felt like a balloon let off a string, absolutely buoyant with relief. The process of writing released that understanding of what the doctor's diagnosis really meant to me.

Other days are humdrum, barren of significance—laundry, bills, letters, picking up after the kids, committee meetings, phone calls for the PTA, lunch boxes to fill, or meals to plan and prepare. Or you're just too tired to think, let alone write. Don't feel guilty if you're not able to write in your journal for a few days. Just pick it up again when you can.

I find, though, that I cannot afford to cut myself off from what I am thinking and feeling for any significant length of time. My friend Margaret Smith, an inveterate journal keeper, once wrote to me: "It's like an enforced fast. If I stop journaling for a couple of weeks I feel weak and numb emotionally and spiritually, out of touch with myself and God."

Some days, I *want* and *need* to write in my journal, yet I'll do anything to avoid it—clean, mend, exercise, organize. That's when it's helpful to set aside a regular time each day for writing—some time when you have been awake and active enough to have something to write about, but you're not too exhausted to pick up your journal and pen. Often writing can, and should, take priority over more "useful" tasks such as cleaning or cooking or cutting the grass.

The reason for an idle or empty journal may be our

In the public arena, my visions of grandeur and heroism swell. The heroic act, the rescue mission, the moment of sacrifice as all eyes register and take notice of the cost. But in the private places, in the scary corners of night, in the folds and creases of self, when only the eyes of self and of God are open, the vision changes. There is no sudden, glorious moment here, only the slow and laborious and frightening process of growth and change.
—Joanie Albrecht, free-lance writer

overcommitment in other areas of our lives, fatigue at the end of the day (even when know we have something important to write), or what we feel is "a boring life." All of us who keep journals go through dry spells, and we can deal with them in at least two different ways.

1. We can wait until we feel the "quickening" of events and ideas in our lives, and simply write what stands out as distinct from the regular routine of life. In other words, we wait "until the spirit moves us," when something happens which is too important to ignore. (I admit this is the route I sometimes go.)

2. We can keep writing regularly, even a few lines a day. It may feel like plowing rocky ground, but in my own experience this discipline is often more fruitful than I anticipate. Even when I open my journal and start to write with nothing important in mind, it's surprising how putting words on paper releases ideas and I find that, after all, something of hidden significance comes to light in the journal process. (I'll say more about this in a later chapter.)

What if you don't know what to write, either through lack of confidence, or ideas, or if you're overwhelmed with life and unsure of everything? *Write that down.* It will help you to clarify and categorize your areas of need. And later, when answers come, or situations resolve, you'll recognize them and make the connection.

Remember—write what you see, whether it is tremendous or trivial. Not only will you gain new awareness and purpose but with practice, you'll see more, and more clearly.

Try this:

1. Think of this past week. Identify some event that seemed trivial but sparked your interest. Write about it in detail. Take lots of time and allow all your senses to inform your writing. As you write, penetrate your topic and let it reveal itself to you. Explore it for possible larger meanings.

"Just don't get caught in the endless cycle of guilt, avoidance, and pressure. When it is your time to write, write."
—Natalie Goldberg
Writing Down the Bones

2. When I'm around _____ , I feel
_____ (fill in the blank). Describe
your feeling about this person, allowing yourself the freedom to tell the truth.

Chapter 5

Capturing Your Life
in Words

Last fall, I sold the home where our family had lived for nearly twenty years. As I was going through cartons of old papers, I discovered a cache of little calendar diaries dating back to my high school and college days, with about five lines for each day of the year.

Of course, I couldn't resist reading them. They brought back some long-forgotten memories. Most of the entries read like this: "Washed hair. Test in Romantic Lit. Met B. for lunch. Letter from mother. Date with H. for Horowitz concert." Or: "Hurt ankle tumbling. Wrote article on 'frustration' for *Kodon* (college magazine). Did layout for *Tower.*" I have to admit I was disappointed; my notes weren't particularly revealing. The basic facts—nothing more.

In the same carton I also found my journals written on a trip to Europe during my junior year in college. These were more discursive and descriptive. For example: "Pub lunch at High Wycombe—steak and kidney pie with cider.

The day is glorious, blue sky, blazing clouds, sun glazing the fields with a glowing enamel green, the larches and beeches in early leaf, lacy and delicate. I want to retain detail. I snap 'mental pictures' scenes or people whose vivid reality I want to print on my imagination."

But they still had little to do with my feelings. (In those days, emotions were not acknowledged very openly by Christians. Feelings were suspect; we were supposed to base our faith and practice solely on *facts*.)

As I read these old diaries, and sorted through scrapbooks, family albums, sheaves of faded letters held together with time-worn rubber bands, I realized how many ways there are, some of them unconscious, by which we keep track of our lives, day by day, week by week. This desire to hold on to past experiences seems to be an almost universal human impulse, though most people don't follow through with it consistently.

◆ Some people keep scrapbooks full of theater tickets, birthday cards, news clippings, postcards, pages from tear-off calendars, notes, memos, foreign stamps, cartoons, ribbons, quotations, award certificates, dried flowers, all of which have special significance to them and serve as memory triggers, reminders of what has happened and why it deserves to be remembered.

◆ A file of personal correspondence, both the letters received and the replies returned, helps us keep track of a friendship or a business relationship.

◆ A family photo album captures for us the actual settings and adventures of our lives, the clothes we wore, our facial expressions, the people we met with, the trips and outings we took together, the parties we gave. Most important, it is evidence of how we grew and changed from year to year.

◆ My husband, John Hoyte, journals with a sketch book, doing
detailed, five-minute sketches
or cartoons of the scenes and
places and people he wants to
remember.

These all have in com-
mon the catching and
treasuring of normal or
joyful or crucial or
intriguing or impor-
tant moments in life. In
a sense, most art forms

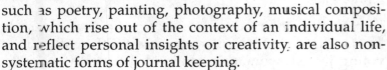

Tomales Bay, on the way to Point Reyes, May 1980

such as poetry, painting, photography, musical composition, which rise out of the context of an individual life,
and reflect personal insights or creativity, are also non-
systematic forms of journal keeping.

Try this:

Think about, and write down some of the ways you
have captured and recorded events and relationships of
significance in your past life. (If you can't think of any
such records, ask yourself *why?*)

Your Journal—A Thread of Continuing Life

You may have received the impression that the only
kind of journal worth keeping is the kind of solemn entry
that deals with spirituality or deep personal crisis.

No. The true journal is *a commentary on all of life*, and
often it is the casual comment, the trivial event that is
shown to be significant as you reread it later. Each day
you live differs in some way from all the others, and your
journal will reflect a diversity of moods and experiences.

Alice Helen Masek, a prolific journal keeper, describes
how it works for her:

"Writing is like a raft that buoys me above the waters of

*"The motivation varies
enormously, but the
urge is the same.
Maybe, at its simplest,
diary-writing is a per-
sonal way of imposing
some kind of perma-
nence or order on the
chaos of the world
around us."*
—Simon Brett, editor
*The Faber Book
of Diaries*

my life, not to keep me from having to swim, but to allow me to gather my breath, plunge deeper and delve for greater riches, then return to the raft for rest and warming, to study and enjoy what I have found on the ocean floor.

"Marine biologists and treasure-hunters on a barge examine their finds from nets and dredges, rinse, sort, classify, and record what is of interest before tossing the rest back in. My writing is 'holding on to the keepers' while sifting the huge mass of information, experience, and reflection that makes up my life.

" 'If I don't write it down, it's gone.' (Was that you, Luci? Or Madeleine? I don't remember. . . . I failed to write it down.)"

In many ways, a journal is a stream of consciousness. In her journal titled *An Interrupted Life*, Etty Hillesum, a young Jewish woman in Holland during the German occupation of World War II, kept a record of her increasingly difficult life as a Jew. In one journal entry she writes:

Such a longing to jot down a few words. Such a strong sense of: here, on these pages I am spinning my thread. And a thread does run through my life, through my reality, like a continuous line. There is the Gospel of St. Matthew morning and night, and now and then a few words on this paper. It's not so much the imperfect words on these faint blue lines, as the feeling, time and again, of returning to a place from which one can continue to spin one and the same thread, where one can gradually create a continuum which is really one's life.

Like Etty Hillesum, I like to keep my journal chronological. That is, I don't divide up my journal entries into categories: sermon notes in one section, poems in another, prayers in another, etc., (though I have to admit this seems to work for some journalers, and I urge you always to organize your journal in the way that seems most comfortable and effective for you). I write in sequence whatever comes into my week—be it sobering, ecstatic, serious, spiritual, literary, trivial, ludicrous, or humorous.

Using dividers or multiple notebooks for different kinds of journal entries tends toward compartmentalizing our lives into separate and distinct functions. Using *only one volume* for all our entries, and writing connectedly, in chronological sequence, has an integrating effect. Our lives *are* all of a piece. You are one person, writing *your story*. It seems both logical and practical to make and keep it a single flow.

Here's an entry from my journal which compares my stream of consciousness with a forest stream in flood:

It has been raining hard here in Sudden Valley. We've had five inches in three days, soaking the ground to a sog, which drains like a full sponge into the creeks. My creek has risen from its customary low profile, a ten-inch wide ribbon of tea-dark water, slow over pebbles, to a super-charged torrent the color of café latte—twelve feet wide and lapping at my house-footings. All night I hear it, my window open to let in the dark sound of rain or river water or a liquid mix of both.

It is like a stream of consciousness. All day and all night it is in the background of my listening and thinking as I write, or stoke the woodstove, or sleep, or make soup. I step out on the deck to check its depth and speed and realize it is myself I am checking. Its flow is so like the flow of my own living and writing—slow and lazy, or full and fierce in the rush of ideas and work. I am writing a stream. I am living a creek.

And alongside the kind of entry just quoted, here are some of the kinds of non-serious journal entries I make (often in close juxtaposition with each other):

◆ Quotes I want to remember from lectures, books, magazines, sermons: From a letter in a new biography of

Georgia O'Keeffe—"The thinking gets more serious when you wonder and fight and think alone."

◆ Titles of the books I have finished reading along with my own comments, or reviews, of those books: *The Contemplative Pastor* by Eugene Peterson. I love his use of the idea of "a Christian subversive"—in this book the pastor subtly effects changes in his congregation by challenging them through the literature of ideas.

◆ Movie reviews: "*Dances with Wolves*—Oh, those wide plains and infinite skies; the human action is both emphasized and brought into its relative insignificance, by comparison with nature. *Bonfire of the Vanities* lacks the power of the book, perhaps because they softened the story line and the consequences of sin."

◆ Jokes, and bumper stickers I want to remember: E.g., "Stop Continental Drift!"

◆ Lists of things to be done, or prayed about, this week: A discussion group to be led, a lecture to prepare, a new neighbor to visit, an editor's deadline to meet.

◆ Interesting place names I notice as I drive across the country. Examples: Crazy Woman Creek, Big Sky, Medical Lake, Boring, Weed, Concrete, Twisp, and the lovely Indian names of the Pacific Northwest: Nooksack, Snohomish, Tulalip, Skagit, Stillaguamish.

◆ Thought-starters—ideas I want to explore when I have more time (how we live in a "crossover world"; how surviving a blizzard makes all of us feel noble, heroic; how any state of mind can draw us to God like a magnet—exhilaration makes us his companions, depression causes us to cry out to him for relief and a lightening of spirit).

◆ Seed ideas, or lines, which may turn into poems; (here's one that is waiting for me to develop it):

The trees are writing lists of leaves,

    The sea a list of waves

"I now record most things which catch my attention: classical music enjoyed on FM radio, clever comments, wise sayings, wry jokes, lecture or sermon notes, timely phrases, vivid descriptions, anecdotes. . . . And, like wildflowers picked on a long and leisurely walk, I marvel at the bouquet."
—Muriel LeBreton, teacher

And I must write a shopping list—
    My have nots, and my haves . . .

Of course, *this* list reflects the kinds of things that appeal to me. Your list may be very different because your life will vary from mine in your interests and circumstances.

Try this:

Make a list of the kind of things you would like to include in *your* journal.

The Varied Uses of a Journal

People write journals in all kinds of ways, for all kinds of reasons. Here are some possibilities:

◆ A young mother, with several children, finds the only time she has for herself is what she calls her "Journal Jog," a kind of spiritual and emotional workout that prepares her to face her busy, fragmented day.

◆ A composer keeps track of his musical ideas and jots down notes—melodies and harmonies—in his musical score journal.

◆ A Bible study leader prepares for a large class as ideas about the Scripture passage for the week occur to her during other activities.

◆ A novelist practices descriptions and snatches of dialogue, and works out his plots, jotting them down as he goes, then typing them into his word-processor.

◆ A university student is having trouble sorting out all the new and conflicting ideas presented in her classes. She uses her journal to record her questions, pray for wisdom, form a world-view that she feels is both biblical and informed.

◆ A busy pastor takes a "journal retreat" for rest, prayer, dreaming, restoration, and personal renewal, using a journal to record the results of this time away from the stresses of pastoral life.

"[My journal] is my garden where seeds are safely planted away from prying eyes, some to grow and take root, others to die quiet deaths."
—Janet Taylor, counselor

◆ A widower puts his grief, his memories of his wife, his struggles with loneliness, his growth as a single human into a notebook.

◆ A college student in a wilderness survival program keeps a daily journal of the stresses, the problem-solving, the physical toughening involved in orienteering. In finding his way across the unfamiliar wilderness, he is discovering how to chart a course for life.

◆ A husband and wife are getting counseling because of a turbulent marriage. During their therapy sessions, and in between, they make notes which highlight their advances in problem-solving as well as their points of conflict. Often in this process they realize what trivial issues are causing disharmony.

My greatest motivation for journaling is that I am saner, wiser, truer, more centered, more conscious, most deeply satisfied, richer, more connected with God and with myself when I write.
—Joanie Albrecht

Try this:

Write your own journal job-description—*your* reason, *your* motivation for keeping a journal.

A journal can also be a practical way of remembering *what happened when* in your past life. Often I ask myself questions such as, *Did I teach that course on imaginative writing in the fall of 1987 or 1988? Was my friend Linda married in the spring or the summer that year? When did I begin to think seriously about remarriage?* If I have a detailed, dated journal I can easily find my answers. At a deeper level, I can retrace emotional journeys in the past, or discover the change-points that altered my spiritual direction.

"[A diary] is always written in the present, and what is written becomes the record of the past, which you read in the future."
—Valerie Raoul

Change-points

Most of us are catapulted into journal writing by changes in our lives:

◆ a new relationship: friendship, engagement, or marriage

◆ the conception or planned adoption of a child; the awareness of the new responsibilities of parenthood

◆ a New Year (complete with resolutions)

- a special vacation or trip

- the move to a new area or job

- a spiritual renewal, or conversion to a new way of believing or understanding God

- the beginning of a new church season, such as Christmas, Advent, Lent, or Easter.

Any of these may energize us and interest us enough that we want to track it in a journal.

Head or Heart?

Journal keeping also answers the often unspoken, or unrealized need in all of our lives for *writing from the heart as well as from the head.* This is what I mean when I talk about "reflective" or "contemplative" writing.

Most of us live our lives as if action—*doing*—is our highest priority, or as if information—*facts*—are the only things worth recording. Attitudes like these are probably a consequence of our technological, data-oriented age. In fact, we get carried along so quickly by the momentum of our own activity and the gathering of data that our time for thinking about the value or significance of what we are so busy about is crowded out.

Journal keeping, the act of writing down what we observe, or think, or feel, slows us down and nudges us to discover the meaning of our lives. In the following chapter we will discuss this in more detail—how we can stop speeding along on the surface facts of life and instead, begin to dive deep and develop a rich, thoughtful, inner life.

"My journal helps me slow down, evaluate. . . . As I am honest on deeper levels in my journal, I am finding that I am less afraid to open myself to people and to confront wrong attitudes in myself."
—Kathy Mann, homemaker

Chapter 6

Inside Out:
Reflective Journal Writing

It may seem odd, but one of the best ways I can slow down my life in order to find a clear, internal focus is to take a fast, two-mile walk in the country. And in moving through this outside space I can, paradoxically, concentrate better on my inner space.

Here's what I wrote after one such morning:

My walk: a cool, mostly sunny day when Fall showed herself unmistakably in the descending leaves—floating straight down the calm air, or rustling in a gust—a long, angled trajectory when the breeze picked up. Whole river banks and yards carpeted, the floors of the forest solid with copper and gold. I found myself humming,

> Hear him, ye deaf,
> His praise, ye dumb
> Your loosened tongues employ!

The trees listen to their Creator. He speaks in seasons,

and they obey. But we humans, with independent minds and wills, are less prone to listen because we cannot be still. When Jesus asked for ears to hear him, he must have longed for human receptacles into which his voice could penetrate and resonate, where his own mind could take root and become part of us. He created. He cares. So he communicates.

Lord, am I allowing this process to happen in me? Yes. All of this morning's meditation is the result of your Spirit interacting with mine to show me, on all levels, who you are, how urgent and ardent is your love.

Defining Our Terms

It may be useful to look at the roots of the key words we're using to describe what happens in a journal.

Think, for instance, about *contemplation*. The Latin word *templari*, from which "contemplation" is derived, means "space"; it's also the root of the word *temple*, which we could describe as "a space prepared for the presence of God." Contemplation could be paraphrased as *spending time in inner space*. And if you are a Christian, your inner space is already inhabited by God's Holy Spirit, so that your contemplation really does take place in his presence and with his help.

Meditation, a discipline that reaches back to the early Christian church, refers to the deliberate shift from purely rational, logical, linear thinking to another level of activity in which the imagination (the part of the mind that sees in pictures or images) has space and time to come into play. Meditation is much like contemplation; it attempts to approach the truth beneath the surface, to penetrate to the center (*media* means middle) of things. Richard Foster uses the Quaker term *centering down*, or *centering in*, to describe the quiet settling of our spirits into a heart-attitude in which true meditation is possible.

"There is sanctuary in these woods, the enclosed spaces with the strong trees protecting the boundaries. I am at home here, I am in church here, silence is natural, reverence is felt, praise erupts. From here I explore the trails, the river, myself, my thoughts, my heart."
—Gail Stevenson, business woman

"For me, being with people . . . for any length of time without solitude . . . I lose my center. I feel dispersed, scattered, in pieces. I must have time alone in which to mull over any encounter, and to extract its juice, its essence, to understand what has really happened to me as a consequence of it."
—May Sarton
Journal of a Solitude

Keeping a journal helps us focus more clearly on what is going on between the outer self and the inner self, and between us and God, as was illustrated from my journal at the beginning of this chapter. As we write, as our fragmented living and thinking becomes more meditative, as we grow still enough to hear, we discover a new sense of integration, resolution, and tranquility.

Try this:

Take a significant moment of your life and reflect on, or "get at the truth beneath the surface," of that moment. Let the moment make some connections for you. Ask yourself: Why did I do what I did? Why did I think what I thought? Have I ever responded like that before? Why? or Why not? What does this incident tell me about my response to life?

Are you ready for more definitions? The words *journal* and *diary* both originate in the Latin word *diurnal,* which means "daily." Some people use the terms *diary* and *journal* interchangeably. Henri Nouwen titled his book *The Genesee Diary.* By contrast, May Sarton's "intimate diary in the year in the life of a creative woman" is titled *Journal of a Solitude.* Both terms, *journal* and *diary,* may refer to daily writing that springs from our outer and inner lives.

However, in this book, when I refer to a *diary,* what I have in mind is a brief record of events and daily data, while *journal* will refer to daily writing that moves beyond the superficial events and becomes a record of responses to those events, personal reactions, prayers, decisions, and a lot more, which enable the writer to get a handle on the significance of those bald facts in terms of personal growth and understanding.

Reflective Writing

Another term for the kind of journal keeping I have found most productive is *reflective* writing.

What does this involve? An analogy may help here: In the same way that animals may think, but they cannot

"As we embrace our reality, we become immersed in God's wisdom, and faith is the eye that we see with. Meditation is the opening of the eye of the heart."
—Gail Stevenson

"Time in silence, in prayer, in dreaming, is essential for true observation and reflection, without which the imagination tends to be inactive or superficial. . . . I don't want to continue in my personal poverty, or try to feed others from my own internal, barren pantry. . . . It is exciting to break out of the box and begin to experience the freedom of discovery in reflection."
—Ruth Stoll, nursing administrator

think about thinking (as humans do, in their self-awareness), so a diary may record, but it doesn't reflect on the meaning of what is recorded.

Let's look at the word *reflective* more closely. Reflecting means *re-flecting*—bending again, flexing inward in self-examination. Elizabeth Fry, a nineteenth century Quaker writer, said, "the advantage of a true journal [is that] it leads the mind to look inward."

Esther Jarratt, a member of one of my summer journal workshops, made this practical suggestion: "As I write in my journal I use only one side of the page. In that way I have space to add and reflect on the facing page. The blank page provides space to list changes, new insights, and resolutions, as well as to ask questions, state connections made in my own thinking, and problems that may have arisen. It allows the words to speak to me and provides space for responses as well as opening me up to God's voice. Reflective writing encourages me to interact with myself as if I were an outsider. I gain a new perspective."

> "Reflective meditation . . . spirals down to deeper layers of meaning rather than moving from point to point. It moves us from head to heart."
> —Susan Muto

Some people worry that such looking inward may lead to morbid introspection, a dark and unhealthy preoccupation with one's own state of mind. But true reflective thinking and writing is not one-directional. After spending time looking into our hearts, we take what we find there, either negative or positive, and express it to God, asking for his response, his correction. In that sense journal keeping is a form of prayer; we are "searching our hearts" in God's presence and asking him to "know our thoughts."

> "Journaling became for me an avenue to prayer, for I could write to the Lord what I could not verbalize aloud."
> —Kathy Mann

Think about your typical early morning routine. You've stumbled into the bathroom, and your sleepy, rumpled image is caught in the surface of the mirror and reflected back to you. It boomerangs, so you can see yourself as you really are (and do something about it). Edward Robb Ellis, in *The New Yorker*, says, "A diarist is a writer who watches himself watching himself."

Of course, at 6:00 A.M. this revelation may be startling. And what you discover about yourself as you write reflectively will not always send you into paroxysms of joy. You will undoubtedly discover flaws and blemishes as you begin honestly to see yourself as God sees you.

For the Christian, reflective writing allows you to *hear* God's "still, small voice," and once you have grown sensitive to its wavelength, attuned to catch his tones with your inner ears, you can go on to *listen to* what God is saying. I noted in my journal: "The voice of God is like a small bird; if you want it to alight on your shoulder you must stand very still."

The Lord speaks to us in so many ways, but many of us have ignored one of his most effective channels—our own thinking, our own minds. In fact, we have been warned *not* to trust our thinking. But if we listen to our reflective minds, and test our thoughts against the standard of God's written Word, there is much to be gained.

Christians often act as if their only worthwhile parts are their souls or spirits. The mind (intelligence) and the body are somehow inferior, and suspect. This is a kind of gnosticism. (The Gnostics believed a heresy in which physical, material reality was seen to be evil, not part of the creation of a good God, and only the soul or spirit was capable of godlikeness.) Within our human personalities body, mind, and soul/spirit need to be integrated, all of them blessed by God and capable of reflecting him.

"I am Body and Spirit as well as Mind. I need all three strands in my River."
—Janet Taylor

In Paul's letter to the Romans we are told about personal transformation "by the renewing of our minds." And, as John Stott has stated pithily, "Your mind matters." As Christians we recognize that we have "the mind of Christ," and the Holy Spirit within us activates that Christ-mind as he "leads us into all truth"—not just abstract theology, not just dogma, but the personal, inner truth about ourselves, and God. The psalmist reminds us in Psalm 16, "The Lord gives me counsel; *my heart teaches me night after night.*"

The Extraordinary Ordinary

Often it's the "ordinary" events that launch us into true, reflective writing. Here, for instance, is a poem I wrote in my journal during a visit from my six-year-old granddaughter, Lauren:

How to Paint a Promise in January

Here in the winter breakfast room,
the light breaks down
as it pushes through
rain-streaked windows, polishing
the wooden table imperfectly.
the colors of the spectrum
are reduced to eight solid lozenges
in a white metal tray. A child's brush
muddies them to gray in a
glass of water.
                    Green leaves always turn
brown. Summer died into the dark days
a long time ago; it is hard even to
remember what it was like
from where I stand now, stalled,
in this narrow slot of time
and light
                Until I look down again,
and see, puddling along the paper
(under a painted orange sun, primitive
as the first spoked wheel)
the ribbon of colors spooling out of
my granddaughter's memory—a rainbow
wide as the sky, arching
over strokes of grass
wet and green enough to be true.

For me, in that dark time of bereavement, a little girl painting a picture took on more than passing interest. Because I reflected on it, I saw something charged with inner meaning in the event. With practice, as you open the inner eyes and ears of your imagination, you will see reality at new and more profound levels. You may write poetry or reflective prose, parables, or simple statements. The form need not concern you as long as you are moving into new territory—your own heart.

Here's a prose example from the journal of Sharon Earl, whose story appears in chapter 1:

> It's Friday the 13th, but such a blessed day for Shep and I—our fifth wedding anniversary. It feels like an indelible mark in my life—so much has happened.
>
> Somehow being married to Shep longer than to Ralph is a milestone for me. The memory of my marriage to Ralph seems very distant . . . maybe that's sad, but it seems to me more a sign of healing and moving on (a tribute to my first marriage).
>
> These past five years have been an incredible journey. The words "arduous but joyous" come to mind. My image of me is that of a tree growing—roots painfully digging deeper into the soil, but then bearing beautiful, leafy branches.
>
> I feel I am truly experiencing the wondrous gift of life God promised me in my "valley of death."—"Your weeping shall be for a night, but Joy comes in the morning."

Observe and Contemplate

I often wonder if Mary, Jesus's mother, might have kept a journal under different circumstances. In Luke 2:19 we are told that following the incidents of the Incarnation "Mary treasured all these things and pondered them in her heart." Mary was a contemplative. Even though she was probably illiterate, like most teenage Jewish girls of her time, she had the reflective heart of a journal keeper—she observed, treasured, and pondered what she saw and heard.

I want to be like Mary. Because you are reading this book I am convinced you want to be like her, too. We all need to be willing to open up our minds and hearts and listen to God in our lives as she did.

Several years ago Madeleine L'Engle sent this out as her Christmas poem:

> Observe & contemplate,
>   make real, bring to be.
> Because we note the falling tree
>   the sound is truly heard.
> Look! The sunrise! Wait—,
>   it needs us to look, to see,
> To hear & speak the word.
>
> Observe & contemplate
>   the cosmos & our little earth.
> Observing, we affirm the worth
>   of sun & stars & light unfurled.
> So let us, seeing, celebrate
>   the glory of Love's incarnate birth
> & sing its joy to all the world.
>
> Observe & contemplate,
>   make real. Affirm. Say Yes,
> & in this season sing & bless
>   wind, ice, snow; rabbit & bird,
> Comet & quark; things small & great,
>   Oh, observe & joyfully confess
> The birth of Love's most lovely Word!

There's our challenge—to observe, to contemplate . . . and to write.

Try this:

Reflect on a specific, recent image or natural phenomenon, bringing all your senses into play as you recall its details. Then begin by writing out a prayer expressing your desire to expand inwardly, asking God to show you an inner vision and use this image to teach you something deep, and lasting. Whatever he teaches you, write.

Chapter 7

Growing with God through Your Journal

Years ago my morning routine would always include this: I'd lie on the floor, tuck my feet under the lower edge of my bureau, and do forty situps.

I was proud of my flat, firm abdomen, until I realized how flabby other parts of me were growing. It wasn't until I got involved in a regular aerobics program in which *all* my muscles got a systematic workout, that my body became an effective, smoothly functioning whole.

It's often the same with the muscles of the mind, soul, and spirit. Because each is a vital part of you, an integrated human, you cannot isolate one from the others and still keep the God-given balance between them.

I made this entry in my journal when I felt a strong connection between my physical exhilaration and the spiritual springtime of my heart:

I started the day with a fast mile walk. The grass, faintly tinged on the sunny slopes with green, glittered in the melting frost. The air was intoxicatingly fresh. Exhilaration. The idea of my being 'dead to sin and alive to God' expanded consciously in my imagination. The air was perfectly still so that the calls and songs of robins and phoebes formed a web of clear sounds all around me as I walked, not muffled or blown away by the strong, spring winds of the days earlier this week. I took my accustomed circuit, finishing up with the curlicue into Wayne Oaks Lane and our driveway. All the way the edges of the turf, the sun-warmed banks and sheltered spots, were brightening with green—spears of grass pushing up through dead, pale straw, and I felt my kinship with the sod.

From my reading in the *Song of Solomon* this morning came the words:

> "My lover spoke and said to me,
> 'Arise my darling, my beautiful one, and
>   come with me.
> See, the winter is past; the rains are over and
>   gone.
> Flowers appear on the earth. The season of
>   singing has come.
> Now birdsong is heard in our land.' "

In an amazing way, the attitude or activity of our bodies affects our thinking, our imagining, our praying. They work together; that's how God planned it.

Walking in the space and freshness of the outdoors stimulates my thinking and praying to new clarity.

Kneeling to pray, in church, or alone by my bed, actually intensifies my prayers.

Standing to sing, with my lungs full of melody, or raising my hands to praise, magnifies my sense of worshiping God.

Physical, emotional, and spiritual realities augment

"Far from being a harsh discipline, journal keeping becomes a condition for the possibility of free, creative self-expression, bringing us into communion with the Personhood of God."
—Susan Muto

each other. For me, the spiritual pervades every part of my life. There are no boundaries between times of Bible study and prayer and other, more "mundane" activities; they're all one, under the grace of God, because I am one, a human being, a single organism whose physical, spiritual, emotional, and mental capacities are given over to him.

From Natural to Supernatural

Digging in the garden, washing the car, writing a letter, joining hands around the dinner table are all real, deserving undertakings in themselves. But they can also become metaphors for other life realities. They are joined to the spiritual truths that rise from them—the cultivation of our hearts' gardens, the need for the cleansing of confession and forgiveness, the communication from God in his letter to us—the Bible, the warm "communion of saints" around the Lord's Table.

Remember how it was when Jesus, after the Crucifixion, met two of his friends on the way to Emmaus? They had trouble recognizing him—perhaps their rational minds refused to believe in resurrection—and it was only as they sat down to eat together—one of the most repeated and ordinary of our daily activities—that "their eyes were opened" and they knew who Jesus was. *Our* eyes may be opened to see Jesus in commonplace things—washing dishes, writing a letter, turning the lights on as evening comes.

Never despise mundane events; they can be doorways to profound spiritual understanding. As my friend, dramatist Kay Baxter says, "Never draw a line between the sacred and the secular unless you wish to deny the Incarnation."

Last year, I wrote in my journal:

In the aerobics group this morning I learned that if you are to avoid getting "out of breath," you have to *keep breathing* deeply and regularly during exercise to

"Journal writing is my pen writing me. It writes about my journey from God and away from him, back and toward him, a stumbling, progressive journey. For me, to write is to trace the threads that hold the person of me on a path that is leading deeper and deeper into God."
—Gail Stevenson

"My definition of journal writing: 1) to walk the pages of your life together with God; 2) to pinpoint significance in daily living; 3) to think thoughts in God's presence; 4) to think about my thinking; 5) to record a day's journey."
—Su Norton, homemaker

"The director of the North Virginia Writing Project pays his students a dollar for every page in their journals. He considers journal keeping that valuable in the development of their personal growth, their informed, reflective personhood."
—Ruth Stoll

maintain the oxygen supply to the heart. And then I began to think of the obvious spiritual parallels—how we need the replenishment of the Holy Spirit to renew our "hearts" with quickening power; the necessity of regular spiritual nourishment if our spirits are to remain as vigorous and healthy as our bodies.

I like to think of life as a flowing river in which each ripple reflects the light from God. My journal gives me a sense of continuous forward movement, of the integrated life in all its diversity.

Seeing Where You've Come From

In my journal writing I have learned the importance of patience, of waiting for God's answers to questions that seem urgent, too important for delay. "Wait" was one of the key words which came to me, again and again, in Scripture, in prayer, in the counsel of friends, during the time I was questioning and searching for the reality of God.

As in the lives of Joseph, Job, David, Mary, sometimes God seems to stand back and leave us in the dark to think through, pray through, work through, grow through our times of crisis. It is not abandonment or a turning of his back. He is there, but silent for a time, like the father in Chaim Potok's novel *The Chosen*. I didn't understand it then, but I do now, as I look back, and read back through old journals.

Several years ago, a pastor in Wichita with whom I met several times about such questions and the future direction of my life was moved to predict in prayer that I would begin "to move in the flow of God's power and pleasure" in me. He went on: "You'll pull out of the vortex of your old repeating cycles of doubt and double-mindedness, and become free and exuberant." Another time he prayed that I would "gain a new confidence, and become *whimsical and free as a little girl on roller-skates.*" Roller skates. I wrote the words down. They were promises for the future as yet unfulfilled, like the special gifts we anticipate for our next birthday.

All that was three-and-a-half years ago. Just the other day I recorded:

Rereading my journal of final days in Wichita I came across Tom Rozoff's prayers for me. I realize they have all been fulfilled—the cycles of doubt and depression have vanished, God is real, I have a wonderful life—productive, free, exuberant, and never boring. And I remembered the song we learned in his church that meant so much to me:

> "I will change your name.
> You shall no longer be called:
> 'Wounded, outcast,
> Lonely, or afraid.'
> I will change your name.
> Your new name shall be:
> 'Confidence, joyfulness,
> Overcoming one,
> Faithfulness, friend of God
> One who sees my face.' "

And now that is all true. There was no dramatic breakthrough. I was just taking small, tentative steps into the dance of life with God, and now I'm dancing with exhilaration and confidence. Because each of those steps was recorded in my journal I can see where I have come from, and I can praise God.

Tristine Rainer writes: "An experienced diarist . . . is willing to place questions in the diary and wait for answers. She trusts the process of the diary, knowing that she has done all she can for the moment in being completely honest with herself.

"Just as you can follow the silvery thread of a garden snail on the grass . . . so on the pages of a spontaneous diary can you observe the characteristic trail of your own

"Sometimes the scribbles and anger and tearstains [in my journal] hardly make any sense. And then, in a quiet moment I'll read over an entry, months old, and shake my head in wonder at the insight, or the healing, or the light softening the sharp and brittle edges of my life."
—Muriel Le Breton, teacher

"As I discover who I am, God is becoming more real to me."
—Kathy Mann

being. . . . Half the benefit of writing lies in completing the process through rereading."

Try this:

Write out any questions you may have about God, prayer, the Bible, your faith. If you are dealing with spiritual knots in your life, here is an opportunity to untangle them.

Joining Journal and Bible

Systematic, devotional Bible study should be a vital element—"food and drink"—for the growing Christian. It is a discipline that works beautifully in conjunction with journal keeping.

As we read Scripture every day, we can record insights gained from our study, our personal responses to God's voice as we hear it in the Bible, and ideas as to how to apply this in realistic and imaginative ways. If we have such a record, it makes obedience to the Word much more possible and practical. It keeps us far more accountable for what we have read, studied, and prayed about.

Ron Klug, in *How to Keep a Spiritual Journal*, says:

"One pastor I know does his sermon preparation in his journal. On Monday morning he chooses the text for next Sunday's sermon. In a spirit of prayer he meditates on the Scripture passage and records his thoughts and prayers. Then on Tuesday he reads what he has written and adds new thoughts. He repeats the process every day. By the end of the week he usually has enough material for two or three sermons. 'It's a way of holding the Word of God for an extended period of time,' he says. 'It helps me sustain myself in the Word and the Word in me.' "

Paraphrasing for Comprehension

Here's another example of how I integrate my study of the Bible with my other journal writing. My spiritual director once gave me the month-long assignment of writing out the "consolations and desolations of life" as I saw them in Isaiah 44. Here's part of what I wrote (like an extended paraphrase of those verses) as I meditated on that passage:

> The God who created and formed me tells me *not to fear*—tells me *not to be afraid* because he has redeemed me. He had to create me twice—once in Eden, and once again in my own time and place to compensate for the pervasive death of the body, and to provide me with a means of survival so that as the body withers, the spirit and soul can bloom and fruit.

> From this second creation, this redemption, this buying back, there can be no withering, no dying back into nothingness. It is a calling, a vocation—"I have called you by name." That name is never generic. It is extraordinarily personal and particular, like a phone call in the evening; not an impersonal business call but a voice of intent sounding on the line, saying, "Don't be afraid. It's me—the one who surnamed you my family name." When God says, "You're mine," there is no sense of a power-hungry tyrant. It's the call of the lover who promises total commitment and asks the same of me. "I want you; you are married to me—body, soul, mind, heart, spirit—all the intermingling, interpenetrating faces of the one who is called human."

> Then comes a stream of promises like water over the lip of the waterfall. "Thirsty land, dry ground," are the conditions we revert to when left on our own. Our naturally arid spirits need rehumidifying by God. His rain-bearing clouds stretch above us, his aquifers lie beneath us. And sometimes we have to wait When our desert is prolonged we feel like giving up, losing hope. What are we here for if not to produce green? But when the rain falls and the green grows at last, it is all the more refreshing by contrast

"God and I walk the pages together."
—Esther Jarratt

"Journal keeping is a way to set spiritual growth goals. Inch by inch we move into the kingdom of God and into the center of His will."
—Shelley Spencer, Member, journal workshop

with the dryness we have known.

During the month when I wrote that, my life was taking some difficult turns and those verses fit my circumstances so perfectly (I'm sure you've had the same experience) that my hold on the Lord was strengthened as I heard his voice speaking through these Scriptures.

Try this:

Choose a portion of the Bible that is meaningful to you (not necessarily a whole chapter; keep it reasonably brief) and paraphrase it (rewrite it in your own words) in relation to your life circumstances. What did you discover that you hadn't realized before?

Praying with Your Journal

You may have noticed that in this book I haven't talked about keeping a "spiritual journal" or a "prayer journal." This is not because I want to ignore the need for spiritual growth, or the vital place of prayer. Rather, it's that I don't want to split off the life of the spirit—my interactions with God—from the other areas of my daily experience.

Perhaps, when praying, you have had a common problem—your mind wanders, your praying becomes fragmentary, you lose track of your conversation with God. Writing your prayers into your journal is a marvelous help in focusing, concentrating, keeping the flow of thought and prayer from breaking off and floating away. There on the page you can see the prayer-words you have already written. Seeing what you have just said to God, and knowing what you still want to tell him, you can continue to write it down.

This has a steadying, stabilizing effect on your prayer life, and on you as a praying person.

Since much of my journal is me reflecting on life and its meaning, it ends up with much of it being my appreciation of God, or questions I am asking him. In my journal I am *thinking my thoughts in God's presence.* I mentioned this earlier; I say it again because it has such a potent reality for me. What better definition, really, is there of prayer? (In one sense, everything we do as God's children is prayer, as we live out our lives before him. Perhaps this is what the New Testament means by "praying without ceasing.")

For you, such an approach to prayer may seem too unfocused, too broad, not purposeful enough. If so, it may help you to find some specific patterns for prayer and meditation that will fit into your journal keeping.

Patterns for Prayer

Here is one prayer model suggested by Karen Mains.[1] (After you have scanned this, take time today to work through it on these pages):

Date and Place (Day, date, year)

Feeling Prayer

This is how I feel today, Lord. . . .

The God Hunt (Where have I seen God in everyday life?)

1. Any obvious answer to prayer.

2. Any unexpected evidence of God's care.

3. Any help to do God's work in the world.

4. Any unusual linkage, or timing.

Housecleaning of the Soul: (confession and forgiveness)

1. Lord, how have I sinned against you, against my fellow humans, against myself? I confess this, and ask for forgiveness.

2. Who has sinned against me? Whom must I forgive?

Praise or Adoration

Lord, this is what I appreciate about you. . . .

Prayers of Request

"I needed to be shown the depth of reflection and personal honesty that is necessary in keeping a spiritual journal. Journaling allows you to get to know yourself and God better, to dig below the surface even if it is painful."
—Shelley Spencer

"There have been times in my life when I've become discouraged because I can't see any progress. It seems like I'm dealing with the same problems and character weaknesses over and over. That's when I write letters to God asking him for his perspective on my static place in life. And in reading old journal entries I see how far I've come; I can see the progress."
—anonymous

1. Lord, I need help with (personal requests). . . .

2: Lord, now I am thinking of others' needs.

Sitting in Silence

Lord, what are you saying to me today? What do you want to teach me?

Another prayer format is based on the acrostic ACTS, referring to:

Adoration (focus on God and his character)

Confession (naming and acknowledging personal failure)

Thanksgiving (verbalizing your gratitude to God)

Supplication (personal requests for yourself and others)

God's Mailbox: Your Journal

If these approaches seem too formal, try writing a daily letter to God. Remember to keep it honest, down-to-earth, unceremonious. God isn't really interested in pious or theological language. He wants to meet the real you, speaking the language most familiar to you. You can't impress him, so why try?

But you can reach him. And a letter in your journal preserves your thoughts and concerns, even your hard questions, for a later time, when you may wish to review your spiritual journey.

Try this:

Write God a letter telling him your reactions to various ideas suggested in this chapter. Ask him to make clear to you which suggestions will work best for you.

Note

1. Karen Mains, "Shortcuts to a Prayer Journal that Works," *Christian Herald*, July/August 1986.

Chapter 8

Dealing with Your Difficulties

Shortly after my first husband's death, I wrote in my journal:

Sunday morning, early. I'm lying here in bed, unraveling at the edges with anxiety. I call out to God for peace and certainty, but none comes. Pressure, pressure is all I feel. The pressures of having to cope with scores of details I feel ill-equipped even to understand—legal documents, investments, a bankbook I can't reconcile. My taxes are overwhelming; I'm cleaned out. Harold, how could you leave me? I'm not ready to be alone.

What am I living for? I feel as if I keep going just to keep going. And I don't have what it takes. I long for centeredness, but I'm pulled outward in a thousand pieces, whirling in centripetal force. People around me think I am strong, brave, whole, giving, integrated. And I have the conviction that I should be. I should have the answers. If I don't have answers at fifty-nine, when will I find them? What is the sense of it all? I have enough questions to fill a bank, but my balance of answers is zero.

I feel so empty.

After church, Sunday. Notes from Chilton Knudsen's sermon today: We can look at the loaves and fishes and see only our inadequate resources for the multitude. *Or* we can look at Christ and his sufficient grace which comes to us in ways we cannot predict, or even imagine, multiplying what little we do have all the way to adequacy and even surplus, excess. This (life) is not a feasibility study. We need not analyze God's means and methods, but simply *let him do it.*

God. You heard me. You understood that I was falling apart. And you sent a messenger with words that help me know you are there to fill in the cracks of my inadequacy. Thank you.

The sense of confusion, of being lost, inadequate, out of control, is a prime cause for emotional breakdown.

My two journal entries voice a heart-cry of need, and the record of how God spoke to that need on the very same day. Having those primal, urgent feelings recorded on paper made both my need and God's response much more real. Having the entries to remind me that God met my need back then allows me to call on him in the future with more confidence. I was reminded that God never tests us beyond our breaking point but "makes a way of escape."

Each of us needs to know that, in a world which seems to pull us in so many different directions, we need not shatter in a thousand pieces. Our busyness, our need to juggle all our activities and responsibilities, "keeping all the balls in the air," often results in intense anxiety.

Is there a way to relieve some of this unbearable tension, without the time and expense of psychotherapy?

"Writing . . . is a way of coming to terms with the world and oneself. . . . [Of overcoming] fear by giving order, measure, and significance to the flux of experience."
—R. V. Cassill
Writing Fiction

Ronald Klug, in *How to Keep a Spiritual Journal*, writes: "I find that after a hectic day or a week loaded with events and people and problems, I gain a great sense of peace by sitting down with my journal in the presence of God and sorting out my life and regaining my perspective. It's like walking around a messy room—toys and clothes and books piled around—and slowly picking things up and putting them in their right places again. . . . My journal helps me sort out things in my life and restore some internal order."

Diffusing, or Defusing, Painful Emotions

Even the saintliest, most secure, spiritual, intelligent, or best-balanced people are caught, from time to time, in circumstances that seem beyond their control—pain, bereavement, abuse, addiction, serious illness, financial struggle, false accusation, spiritual dryness, personal conflict, doubt, fear, depression. Does any of these ring a bell for you?

These are feelings that must be faced and resolved, or at least lived through in the hope of future resolution. It doesn't help to bury problems; I have friends whose method of dealing with such problems is to ignore them, hoping they will "just go away," and the painful feelings with them. Others (I include myself) have the opposite tendency—to "catastrophize" difficulties, allowing them to loom so large in our minds that we can no longer handle them, or see them in perspective. As we do this, our fears and anxieties become irrational, and begin to go out of control, drastically affecting our ability to make wise decisions, or live "normal" lives.

Many counselors recommend that their clients in both categories—the ones who deny their problems as well as those who magnify them—keep a journal. For one thing, when we describe our problems in realistic detail in journals, as they occur, as well as our responses to them, we can see them better for what they truly are.

"If everyone journaled regularly and deeply, there would be less traffic to psychotherapists."
—Janet Taylor, counselor

"Writing down thoughts and feelings and rereading them later, I watched the jumbled pieces of my life start to fit together. I was able to feel my pain, then write about it. . . . With words I took the pain and turned it inside out, upside down and back again, only to come back to it and go through it all over again. Sometimes I wondered if I could ever leave it behind, but the process felt so right that I kept at it. Like Naaman I had to bathe in the river not once but seven times.

"Finally a day came when I looked over old entries and the pain was gone. I had said goodbye."
—Su Norton

As Christian psychologist Dr. Anne Huffman says: "When it comes to problems, the way *out* is the way *through*." One excellent way to work *through* the problems is in our journals. The pain of enduring, or denying, problems may destroy us, but the pain of engaging them brings healthy growth. If we tend to deny our difficulties, writing them down reminds us that we haven't yet resolved them. If they are like Giant Despair in our lives, as we journal them they shrink from gigantic to life-size, much as the "terrors of the night" (to use Walker Percy's phrase) become far less terrifying by morning light. Journal-keeping helps us realize that our denial, or our panic, is out of proportion to the problem.

A journal gives us an outlet for pent-up emotion and a more reasonable perspective on ourselves and our feelings. Journal writer Mary Campbell says: "Sometimes just writing it down gets rid of a painful problem. I haven't said it vocally, but I've said it emotionally. It takes the load off."

When I am feeling emotional pain, pain that is almost unbearable, I have learned to express it in words on my journal page. Once I write out the pain it seems to draw the sting out of it and make it bearable. *There is the pain on the page.*

Try this:

In a quiet time and place, ask God to give you a picture, or metaphor, of your pain. Does it have a color, shape, or texture? Can you feel it somewhere in your body? Write what you learn from this word-picture.

Negative Emotions?

When a surge of anger breaks like a wave inside us, flooding us, shaking us to our roots, we may become so afraid of our anger that we become paralyzed and guilty.

It is human to have strong negative feelings—rage at someone who has cheated us, fury about a broken promise, frustration with someone who stubbornly refuses to see our point of view—even when such anger is justified, the real difficulty comes in expressing those feelings appropriately.

Rather than allowing your anger to be vented in a form of physical or verbal attack, it may be expressed honestly, freely, privately, and safely, on the pages of a journal. Your writing becomes a safety valve, a vent for your pent-up emotional steam. No one but you and God need know the intensity of your anger.

If you're struggling with pain and the need to forgive someone, rather than saying or doing something you might regret later, write a letter to that person. Assume that he/she will never read the letter, and be very honest about your feelings and descriptions.

Once you have used your journal to describe your feelings in writing, and you see them in context for what they are, you can determine what to do about the situation: whether or not bringing the past to God for forgiveness and healing will suffice, whether or not to take action, whether or not to confront the person causing your violent reaction.

You've had your say, you've come to understand and articulate the conflict and its causes, but no one has been hurt. You have canceled the probability of an on-going feud.

In writing about your feelings, you will come to realize whether or not they fit the circumstances that caused them. This will help you to deal with the whole situation more reasonably.

Writing What You Feel

When you are feeling resentment, or some other negative emotion, or if you are undergoing some trying experience, it may be helpful to describe in detail just what your internal mix is.

"Being totally honest was new and freeing for me. I've always written with the thought of someone looking over my shoulder. It was incredibly good for me to 'let it all out' on paper."
—Sharon Earl

I'm an impulsive person. Here's how I felt about *having to wait*:

Waiting is full of tension, frustration, fear, hunger. I am a bunched bundle of neck and shoulder fibers waiting for sleep, an orphan waiting for a visit from the Father, a wind-harp waiting for a breeze to end my muteness, a letter waiting for a stamp so I can go somewhere. Waiting is the word that shows my state, tells my story.

On the other hand, our most positive emotions deserve expression, too.

This is what *joy* felt like to me:

Joy is a feeling that starts in the chest and spreads, showing its strength in the angle of the head, the shape of the mouth and the lines on each side, and the way the eyes open. It is a fullness that wants to run, shout, break down barriers for God, hurdle boundaries. Sometimes it simply wants to sit still, glowing like a coal that can't afford to lose heat. Joy is addictive—a drug of the spirit.

Ambiguities

What about feelings of ambiguity and self-contradiction? Don't insist on clarity: it's unlikely that you can sort everything out and come to clear cut resolutions about all the paradoxes in life.

None of us is totally integrated or single-eyed. Yet. We must learn to live with a certain level of ambiguity in this world, with all its good and all its evil, and with the mystery of the unknown.

But writing will help us sort out the contradictions we see within ourselves—contradictions like: "I know I am a gifted person, yet I doubt my own worth"—and to work through them and begin to find a foundational integrity before God. When we are wrestling with God, as Jacob did, we are at least in close contact with him. Each waffle or bobble is contributing to a larger or deeper sense of what is true, real, like multiple rivulets contributing to a stream.

If you're writing ambiguities, at least you'll know you are being honest. And that is one of the first steps to emotional and spiritual wholeness.

Ask yourself: Am I willing to look at my dark (or shadow) side? One way is to begin observing your behaviors, feelings, or thoughts that seem to be compulsions. These may trap you in a mode of drivenness and addictiveness—really a form of emotional slavery.

Try this:

Ask yourself, and write your answers here or in your journal: What do I want to be free from? What am I running from? What am I running toward? Is there a need underneath that I sometimes barely glimpse? What would happen if I gave that need a voice and let it speak for itself? How do I respond now to what it is telling me? I have a choice, to listen to it, or smother it. Which will I do?

Working through the Past

Sometimes past events drastically affect the present. But attitudes that are the result of old wounds, negative feelings about the people in our lives, may begin to be dealt with through journal writing.

In a journal workshop I led in British Columbia, several of the participants found their journals to be catalysts for healing. Here are some of their comments:

"You have pain and you deal with it in your journal. You also have to deal with the memory of the pain. And again, your journal becomes your counselor,"—Muriel LeBreton.

"I had never before considered using my journal as a form of therapy and personal release. I wrote in my notes,

"Some things seem too awful to acknowledge, or our reactions too violent to believe. Once I became honest I could write the realities. Not easily—it takes courage; but admission is the first step. Denial accomplishes nothing."
—Kathy Mann

'I'm scared at how deep I may have to dig.' From that point on I began to see how much I had hidden behind a mask so people could not see what I really felt."—Shelley Spencer.

"I'd received a phone call. It gave no particular news nor informed me of anything negative. And yet as I walked away . . . in many replays I heard again the tone of voice, the words, the responses, the possible explanations, over and over. It was when I spied my journal that I began to articulate on paper the feelings. I had allowed this small phone call to rob me of my joy. I poured out the whole lot on the pages of my journal, and it proved to be the fastest way to stop the downward spiral of unhealthy thought. As I laid aside my journal I was aware of the calm within. Journaling had created the space,"—Esther Jarratt.

"[The journaling retreat] reemphasized to me my need to keep the emotions flowing. I need that regular space and flow in my life,"—Ann Long.

While this chapter cannot deal exhaustively with how to cope with present trauma and with the healing of old wounds, I hope you now have some ideas about using your journal as an agent of resolution when you encounter difficulty (as we all will) in your life.

Try this:

If you are sometimes aware of a "wounded child" within you, find a photograph of yourself as a child and begin to look at it as if for the first time. What is the child feeling? Needing or wanting? Trying to say? How do you feel toward the child? Give the child a voice to speak to you, and to God, perhaps in dialogue.

Or think of your life as a candle flame. When you see its small light in your imagination is it against a dark background? Are other candles burning near you? Is the air around you peaceful or turbulent? What shadows surround you? What winds or rainstorms threaten to blow

your candle out? When you have identified these bless-
ings, or perils to your wholeness and safety, write how
you feel about them, and then pray for God to show you
what you can do to keep your candle burning.

Chapter 9

The Writer's Notebook

"Please, could you turn off the fluorescent light? I'm allergic to it." That was my introduction to Della (not her real name) as she sat in my office, looking at me with frightened eyes, like a wounded bird.

I had been assigned as her supervisor in an independent, post-graduate study. It was thought that a journal keeping approach to her academic studies would help her overcome her nervousness and help us recognize the blocks that were preventing her from completing courses.

Della was a highly intelligent but emotionally damaged woman, a missionary returned from the field following a breakdown. She was eager to work through a number of difficult issues in her life, including abuse in her childhood, and an extreme case of low self-esteem. Hampered by innumerable health problems, and a victim of chronic fatigue, she admitted she often felt suicidal.

After our first interview I gave her a book on spiritual

direction and another on journal keeping, asking her to read them, then write in her journal her responses to them, and any memories from the past triggered by reading them.

At our next meeting, when I asked how her journal writing had progressed, she hesitated, then pulled out of her folder three sheets of paper which she handed to me very self-consciously.

She had written three poems. As I read them, I was amazed at their vivid imagery, their concrete, sensuous detail, their penetration and insight. I asked her, "How much poetry have you written?" Her answer: "None. This is the first time I've ever tried poetry. But as I wrote in my journal last night I began to remember things from the past. I could see the scenes, the people. My words began to form poems."

I told her how impressed I was with her writing, and for the first time I saw a look of genuine pleasure and happiness transform her face. She had something to be proud of! Journal keeping, and the images and words it freed in her, had revealed her own unsuspected gift.

As we continued to meet, and talk, and pray together, we both saw ways in which her giftedness could be used by God and be one key for personal transformation. Of course that wasn't the end of her problems, but her journal gave her a way of feeling happy about herself and of processing her pain, as well as of honing her writing skills.

The Writer's Responsibility: To Catch the Truth in a Net of Words

Because language is a uniquely human activity, and because we are human, *we are verbal thinkers.* Yet I have been fascinated to realize, as I write, that thinking often follows or accompanies writing rather than preceding it.

Dorothy Sayers said, "We have no way to think except in pictures." She is right. But our mental images are so

"As your write in your journal, you will develop greater ease and fluency in your writing. This may one day lead you to try writing for publication in a magazine or local newspaper, or even to write a book. A journal is a great training ground for the writer, and the experiences and thoughts captured there can be the raw material for many articles and stories."
—Ron Klug, in
How to Keep a Spiritual Journal

fleeting, so fragmentary, that to bring them into the realm of consciousness and thought we must catch them in a net of words, like butterflies.

W. H. Auden asks: "How do I know what I think until I see what I say?" In this process of spoken or written verbalization we discover what we are really thinking; what has been fleeting or chaotic in our thinking. A mere gleam of truth, easily lost, becomes concrete and available and immediate as we write it into words.

Many writers have experienced, as I have, this eerie sense that in writing we are putting down realities we knew already, but *never knew we knew*!

Annie Dillard says, "Seeing is, of course, very much a matter of verbalization." Until we write, or speak about what we see, we may not know what it is, or why it is important.

Poet and essayist Denise Levertov says, in *The Poet in the World*, "The poet does not see and then begin to search for words to say what he sees: he begins to see and at once begins to say or to sing, and *only in the action of verbalization does he see further*. His language is not more dependent on his vision than his vision is upon his language." Elsewhere, she tells us, "If one is a poet, then the envisioning, the listening, and the writing of the word, are, for that while, fused. . . . In mulling over what I knew I felt and thought, I had stirred up levels of imagination of things I did not know I knew, which made it possible for the poem to emerge in metaphor."

Writer Susan Griffiths echoes this idea. In her essay *Thoughts on Writing: A Diary*, she tells us, "Each time I write, each time the authentic words break through, I am changed. The older order that I was collapses and dies. . . . I do not know exactly what words will appear on the page. I follow language. I follow the ideas and the sounds of the words, and I am surprised and transformed by what I write."

"That self-conscious narrator in me [is] afraid to get out of the way because I have no control at that moment. I have no idea what it might say, where it might lead, how it might make me, and others, feel. To trust your own story is really a brave act. It requires a kind of surrender, believing that it can, after all, tell it better than you can."
—Joanie Albrecht

"To sit down and just write and find out thoughts that I didn't know I had and to trust the Holy Spirit's work in this process is scary, but exciting."
—Sharon Earl

"Transformed by what I write"—what more can a journal writer wish! Our journals can become means of God's grace to us!

If you are a writer (or want to become one) or if you want to be more open to ideas, and truth, and grow in your human awareness, you must heed experienced writers who tell you how necessary it is to put your ideas into writing, to catch them securely in the net of words.

Here an example of how an idea developed as I wrote about it:

Yesterday someone asked me for my definition of "success." A good question.

I believe that a measure of success is essential in the formula for human living. But the more I think about it, the more I am convinced that succeeding (in the most common sense of the word) may be either destructive or healthy, depending on what motivates it. Our culture urges us, always, to do better, to be better, to be competitive, to win the pennant, to take home the biggest Christmas bonus, to pick up a Pulitzer, or at least to raise the most self-confident children. Such success is nearly always pride- and ambition-centered.

And it's addictive. Achievers need a regular "success fix."

Does the Bible endorse success? Yes, but of a different kind. In spite of adversity, Joseph climbed the success ladder not because he was aggressive and pushy but "because the Lord was with him and made him prosper," and "gave him success in everything he did." Joshua 1:8 promises us that we will be "prosperous and successful" if the Scriptures are central in our lives. When we are moved upon by God to be obedient, and achieve a goal that furthers his kingdom, success has an eternal dimension.

A Model for Writing

Here's what Henri Nouwen says in *The Genesee Diary*: "At times, writing becomes a real event. During the last few days I have been worrying about how to write on the prayer of the heart. I reread different books on the prayer tradition of the desert fathers . . . but I still felt uneasy, not really ready to write. Today I simply decided to *start* and see what would happen. After the second sentence it seemed as if my pen pulled me into a totally different direction than I had expected, and while I wrote one page after another, I realized that my concentration on the desert fathers had kept me from thinking and writing about more important things which fit better into the totality of the book I am trying to write. It was a remarkable sensation to see ideas and words flowing so easily, as if they had always been there, waiting."

Nouwen's experience provides a model that we can translate into good advice. Don't wait to "be inspired" to write. Start. Take pen in hand. Put pen to paper. Allow the flow of marks on paper to become a flow of ideas. Learn, in the words you write, what you are really seeing and thinking, what God really wants you to say, what truth is being shown you in your own experience.

I have heard many aspiring writers say, "I've always wanted to write; I *know* I have a book in me." The difference between the writer and the aspiring writer is that one has acted with purposefulness on the inner impulse to verbalize and record what he or she sees, and one has not.

> "Artistic growth is, more than it is anything else, a refining of the sense of truthfulness. The stupid believe that to be truthful is easy; only the artist knows how difficult it is."
> —Willa Cather

Writing and Reading

There are no shortcuts along the track to becoming a good writer. Three basics are: Write, write more, and rewrite!

But reading is vital, too.

As we read good literature we accumulate an understanding of how words work, how vivid, authentic

> "True ease in writing
> Comes by art,
>   not chance,
> As those move easiest
> Who have learned
>   to dance."
> —Alexander Pope

language communicates; we acquire a *feel* for style. There is no more effective route to developing a good prose style than reading widely and hungrily.

In your development as a writer you may find yourself imitating many of the diverse styles of today's great writers before finding your own true voice. In this your journal will be an invaluable aid as you experiment and listen to the sound of your own writing. (One of the best tests of writing is to read it aloud. Weaknesses or flaws in style or logic or consistency will show up when you hear the cumulative sounds of the words.)

Don't waste your time reading pulp fiction. Read the great works of literature—novels, poetry, essays, plays. Read the magazines of news events and ideas. Not only will your style be developed; your imagination will be fired, your store of information and understanding broadened. Each of us can live only one life. But by reading the experience of others we can live a thousand lives vicariously.

Moments of Awareness

Journal keeping is a highly creative way of encouraging ourselves to observe and describe more carefully and thoughtfully the people, events, adventures that swim into our lives. We want to catch the "extraordinary ordinary," the moment when we are suddenly made aware that we are seeing something significant.

As a writer I practice describing the places and individuals I pass. (Did you think I seemed a little preoccupied when we were talking together? I was probably thinking how I would describe you!) When I come up with an interesting or apt phrase I write it down in my journal. When I have an idea that needs to be enlarged or developed, I write it in my journal. I record snatches of dialogue. I copy quotations. Any or all of these may reappear later in a book or an article or a poem.

Keep it Detailed

What makes most writing come alive? Vivid, concrete, detail. Beginning writers often try to move into the large, overarching issues of life and end up using indistinct generalizations that are too fuzzy to keep a reader's interest.

Instead of talking in a broad, abstract way, or with flowery sentimentality about seeing an aged parent decline, and realizing that her life flows into a new generation, notice how I let the small particulars of my mother's room in a nursing home tell the story, and bring home, concretely, the truth of dying, and living.

At the nursing home
for my mother

As seeds swell, they shape and split
their pods. On the cold linoleum
under the bed her molded slippers lie,
slight as a child's, like discarded
seed cases. Long ago
her genes were sown into our soil.
Now she is shrunk all over,
a leaf separating, curling in.

The curtains are always drawn;
after cataracts she shuns
the glare of the world (gardens blaze unseen
on the other side). Her geraniums,
in pots along the sill, are dying
for lack of light, their petals blood-dark.
The only colors in the room
bloom in the framed photographs
we give her every year: from the wall
the dresses of her four great-granddaughters
glow bright as flowers—
iris, poppy, periwinkle, marigold.

Try this:

1. This week, listen for dialogue or cogent quotations

"When my thoughts were vague, hazy, my journal acted like binoculars to bring the blurred image into focus."
—Su Norton

"It is a good deal easier for most people to state an abstract idea than to describe and thus recreate some object that they actually see, they are concerned primarily with unfleshed ideas and emotions. . . . They are conscious of problems, not of people, of questions and issues, not of the texture of existence, of case histories and everything that has a sociological smack, instead of all those concrete details of life that make the actual mystery of our position on earth."
—Flannery O'Connor

that trigger your thinking. Record them, and then write more, wherever your thoughts lead you.

Or:

2. Without thinking too long, select four nouns (names of things), four adjectives (descriptive words), and four verbs (words of action). Write them down, and use them in an original, detailed, written portrait of your own hand. Take ten minutes for this exercise.

And:

3. List the books you have read in the last month, with a brief review of each. How balanced, and how broad, is your reading?

Writing Metaphorically

Shortly after my husband's death, I wrote this in my journal:

> Last Sunday I did a funny thing in church. On impulse, I took the wedding band and our twenty-fifth anniversary ring and diamond off my left hand and tried it on my right. My surface reason was that I wanted to see what it looked like. Unfortunately, once I'd urged the rings into place over the joint, they gripped; I couldn't get them off again. They're still there, a week later, which means that they've felt strange, knobby, bulky all week, and that has reminded me, forced me to think more deeply, about why I moved them.

> I think it was because the rings gave me and others the false impression that I was still married, a normal wife and partner—everything comfortable and companionable and settled. And it was a dishonest statement, because I'm solitary, a single anomaly in a married world. I love my rings. H. and I chose and designed them together. . . . But my rings are a symbol of what *was*, memorials, not signs of present reality.

To change rings from hand to hand seems a simple thing. Unsensational. But my left hand refuses to forget, and six days later around the ring finger is a channel of pale, untanned skin where the gold has pressed its shape into me for all my married years. I feel that there's a similar invisible scar of love around my heart.

(From *God in the Dark*.)

Later, when I had built a cabin in the woods of the Pacific Northwest, I wrote about the new stove that heated the place.

Writing is like making a fire in a woodstove. You don't do it as an off-the-cuff, occasional hobby. If it is to warm your soul and others' souls with a steady flame, preparation (collecting the kindling of ideas and images) and dedication (feeding wood into the stove regularly to keep the flame from going out, disciplining yourself to write with consistency) is the price you pay.

These two examples from my own journals show how we can discover *metaphors of life* in the most mundane circumstances. As I write the wedding rings on my finger and the fire in the woodstove have meaning beyond themselves. They aren't "just" rings or a stove. They carry my thoughts into other arenas and illuminate me.

A metaphor, or word-picture, because of its vividness and reality in one realm of life can *carry over* that meaning, transporting it into another realm. (I have just learned that the modern Greek word for moving van is *metaphoros!*)

A metaphor compares *this* with *that*. There are correspondences between physical and spiritual reality. The wedding ring is more than decorative jewelry; it is a symbol for marriage. The woodstove does more than keep the house warm; it speaks to me of some parallels between the care and feeding of woodstoves and the disciplines of writing.

The Bible is full of metaphors—a thirsty deer, a vine, a tree on a river bank, a shepherd and his sheep, a well of water, bread, wine, light, oil, a treasure in a clay pot. The natural world may suggest other metaphors that enrich our lives. My personal metaphors for living have included the green of growing plants, the shore and the sea, sailing, quilting, knitted sweaters, even Romanesque and Gothic architecture!

My friend Amy Harwell has terminal cancer. She wrote a book called *When Your Friend Gets Cancer: How You Can Help* (Shaw Publishers). In it Amy tells us:

> Not only can I now cope with my broken parts, I can accept the line in the Lord's prayer: *Thy will be done.* I knew I had reached this acceptance of God's will one day as I was driving down a country road. A tree caught my attention—a beautiful pine with lush, spreading boughs. Or it would have been—but all the branches had been sheared away on one side to allow the phone wires to pass.
>
> I am that tree. Because God had other plans for me, I was pared away here and there to let loving messages come through to others.

Thinking and writing metaphorically has helped Amy to make sense of a desperate situation in life and see its place in the pattern of the whole.

No matter what your circumstances, you will be enriched as you become aware of metaphors that apply to your life.

Try this:

Scan the following list of metaphors from the Bible and nature or find your own word-picture in the psalms or the parables of Jesus.

- ◆ oil lamp (2 Corinthians 4:6-7)
- ◆ clay pot (Jeremiah 18:4-5; Romans 9:20-21)
- ◆ candle or lamp (Matthew 5:14-16)

- salt (Matthew 5:13)
- garden (Isaiah 61:11; Jeremiah 31:12b; Hosea 14:5-8)
- gardener (1 Corinthians 3:6)
- someone looking in a mirror (James 1:23-25)
- Body part (I Corinthian 12)
- fragrance of Christ (2 Corinthians 2:15-16)
- fisherman of people (Mark 1:17)
- fruitful vine (Psalm 128:3)
- branch of the Vine (John 15:5-8)
- deep-rooted plant (Ephesians 3:17; Amos 9:15)
- healthy tree (Psalm 1:3, 52:8, 92:12-14; Isaiah 61:3;
    Jeremiah 17:7-8; Matthew 7:17; Colossians 2:6)
- field, forest (Isaiah 32:15)
- messenger (Isaiah 57:12; Nahum 1:15)
- temple, home for the Holy Spirit
    (1 Corinthians 3:16-17)
- sower of seed (Luke 8:11)
- treasure seeker (Matthew 13:44-45)
- crown (Isaiah 62:3)
- bride (Isaiah 62:5; 2 Corinthians 11:2)
- water channel (Isaiah 58:11b; Psalm 107:35-37)
- sheep (Psalm 23:1-4)
- thirsty deer (Psalm 42:1-2)
- field, beach, shell or pebble, seed, river, leaf, river,
    mountain, fruit, pool, pearl, ship, garment, pilgrim,
    athlete, farmer soldier

After you have made a choice, read the Scripture passage thoughtfully and thoroughly, or meditate on the natural image that feels most alive to you, that fits you, your personality, your circumstances, your gifts. Be quiet before God, giving him time to reveal new aspects of your identity to you through the imagery you have chosen.

With your notebook, notice what the words of Scripture look like, smell like, feel like, taste like. Examine its context—its dynamic relationship with its surroundings.

Investigate, in your imagination, its function and value, and its emotional impact on you. Keep it real—don't let it

*"Metaphor has allowed
me a whole new way to
relate to and under-
stand God, and to
make sense of life. I
find myself actively
looking for metaphors
now."*
—Sharon Earl

become abstract. Let it print itself on your imagination.
Write what you discover.

This is a time of being still, and receiving from God.
Give him time over the next days or weeks, and let him
speak to your deep heart.

1. Now, write a job description of yourself in terms of
the metaphor (word-picture) you have chosen. Ask yourself how your personal, spiritual gifts, and/or natural
abilities fit you for this model. If you live out this image,
what might be the results in your own growth? In the lives
of those close to you? In your church community? In the
world around you?

Or:

2. Write a psalm or prayer of praise, making use of all the
ideas suggested by your metaphor. Try a word-association
exercise—list all the words that come to mind in connection
with your metaphor. Use these, where appropriate, in your
psalm or prayer. Don't be afraid to free your imagination—let it enrich your thinking and writing, even if it
sounds different from anything you have written before.

If you have privacy, pray back to God what you have
written, *aloud*, asking him to make it even more real to you
so that it will inform your growth, your decisions, your
life path into the future.

———— ◆·⊪═◄◆〉�‹◖◉◗›◄〉◆►═⊪·◆ ————

Earlier, I promised to tell you why my journal has
become more to me than just a notebook—how God has
used it, twice, as a symbol of what is most valuable, most
precious, in my life. I will let the words written in the journal itself tell most of the stories.

The setting of the first incident is Regent College in
Vancouver, B.C., where I was then teaching poetry as
Writer in Residence.

Tuesday, November 8 At the Faculty Retreat yesterday morning Jim Houston addressed us on "The Amateur (lover for the love of it) Status of the Christian Life." His thoughts raised in me, once again, the passionate questions, "What is God about? What does he want of me?" I told Jim I needed to spend time with him.

Next morning, he came to my office, sat down and said without further introduction, "I know that often in your life you have felt abandoned: by a preacher father who was away most of the time, by insensitive friends, by Harold, whose death has left you alone, and by God.

"My conviction is that you will find an answer to your feeling of abandonment only in *self-abandonment*, in a willingness to relinquish yourself, your identity, to God. For years, now, you've been walking through a long, dark tunnel. Soon you will see light ahead of you, and when you emerge from the tunnel you'll find yourself on the edge of a cliff." (All this time, I was listening almost open-mouthed. Jim knew me well; we were good friends. But how could he speak with such certainty? His voice had the solid ring of prophecy, yet I was hardly ready for what he said next.) "You must throw yourself off the cliff edge and trust that God will catch you in his arms."

A startling charge. It made me shiver, not only with the chill of dismay but with the recognition of truth. I must take this instruction seriously. But I needed time to think through *how* this was to happen. *How* was I to throw myself off this metaphorical cliff?

Jim's word *abandon* appealed to me. All my life I'd been urged by spiritual mentors to "yield," to "surrender all" to God, to "relinquish" what was most dear. These words had become cliches which had lost their force and their emotional edge for me, but the wildness, the "all-or-nothing-ness" of the word *abandon* challenged me to take this new risk, for God's sake, and for my own.

Tuesdays, Regent people get together in small groups to pray at lunch-time. Journal in hand, I went out to my car with Laurie, a young mother, her baby, and the baby's stroller, which I loaded into the trunk. We drove to the nearby home where our group met, and on arrival I realized, with a jolt of alarm, that my journal was gone.

My journal is an extension of me, as important, in its way, as an arm or leg. Or an eye. In it (the current volume was three-quarters full) I feel my life condensed, myself embodied; my most personal observations and ideas and reflections are recorded in it like the path of my life. There was no way I could reconstruct all that detail from the past months. I could buy another journal, but its new pages would be blank.

Troubled, I rushed back to campus in the car and checked my office, then followed my trail through the building and out again to the parking lot. No journal. As I walked back to my car in a light rain I felt the interior tremor, the beginning recognition of what this loss really meant. It was like losing my self. *Losing myself.* . . . Suddenly I realized what was happening—God was claiming my sacrifice. He was telling me the *how* of abandonment.

I gulped, then found myself saying, inwardly, "Lord, this is almost too painful to think about, but yes, if my journal stands for what you want of me, I give it up to you. I abandon it. I throw myself over the cliff. But please, be there to catch me!"

Still shaking, I drove myself back to the prayer group. As I pushed open the front door Laurie met me and said, beaming, "Karen Cooper just phoned to say she'd found your journal in a puddle in the middle of University Avenue. You can pick it up at her house this afternoon." (As I drove away from Regent the journal must have fallen off the car roof where I'd put it while stowing the stroller in the trunk.)

Later, when Karen, my student and friend, handed me the soggy journal, I saw a tire print stippled across its familiar, ugly, orange cardboard cover. Its back cover was ripped off. Its pages were damp and creased, its ink blurred, its coiled wire spine was bent and flattened. But it had been given back to me.

I had made the leap from the cliff. God had made the catch.

Karen and I prayed in amazed gratitude. Then she murmured, "And some people doubt the personal involvement of God in their lives? Why should I, who knew you well, and knew where to find you, have been the one to stop my car in the rain and find out what was lying on the street? Why did I stop at all? Traffic was heavy. There were scores of cars and bikes and pedestrians. But I picked up the journal, and saw your name written on the front."

In my recovered journal I wrote the story that night, and its conclusion:

"If I am willing to abandon myself to God, he will give me back myself, my identity. My will may be broken like the wire coil of the journal, my cover may be imprinted with God's own tire-track signature, but that just proves again that he does care for me, and wants me for himself."

The second incident was written a year and a half later, a few days after I had met John Hoyte. Following a meeting arranged by Tom and Karen Cooper, we had spent most of four wonderful days together in Vancouver, and both felt the unspoken promise of the future. Then I had left for some international council meetings in Bangkok, followed by visits to India and Australia, and was scheduled to be away for a month.

The morning I left, my journal records:

Saturday A.M. John called me, 9:00 A.M. to read Ephesians 3:14-21 to me as a blessing over my trip. Then he prayed, for me, for peace, for safety, for health. I felt strengthened by this scarf of prayer wound around me and my life.

En route to Seattle. I feel so tender—my heart is full of emotion that rises quickly and bursts in my eyes, my face, like coffee bursting up and running down in a percolator. I find myself praying, with a sense of flow between God and me—the quickness and aliveness of relationship, of connectedness. . . . I'm trying to discern in prayer whether I should call John in California during my layover in Seattle.

SeaTac airport. Noon. I called John and caught him in the middle of a Bible study with a medical student friend. I could tell that the presence of another person constricted him. He was cordial but not as personal or intimate as in our other conversations. I think the call was frustrating for us both, and I hung up with a sense of disappointment, sorry I'd called after restraining myself from phoning last night and feeling disciplined and noble.

Now I have been escorted out to the Thai Airlines terminal in the international satellite of the airport.

Later. I reached into my bag for my journal, to write about the abortive phone call—and it wasn't there. I felt sick, almost sure I had left it on the American Airlines plane from Chicago. I tried to call American on the pay phone and gave up after all my quarters were gone and I still hadn't reached the right extension. Time was short. I felt rising panic and kept wondering, "Is this loss of the journal a sign I need to relinquish something? Maybe this new relationship with John?" I felt an inner certainty that the answer was "Yes," that I needed, once again, to give up the journal, and John, to God. So I did. Not easily, but I felt I had no alternative.

By then it was nearly time to board for Bangkok. Suddenly, surprisingly, I heard my name on the loud-speaker. I went over to the Thai podium, as requested, and a young woman asked, "What's your name?" When I gave it she handed me . . . my worn, green journal. I felt overwhelmed with relief, but had, and still have, no idea how they found it, or me. How did the journal make its way out to the international satellite just in time? How would anyone know where I was, even if they read my name on the journal's cover? The whole affair seems not only mysterious but miraculous.

Now I ask myself, "What does this mean?" I'm working through this as I write it, here on the plane over the wide Pacific, with marbled clouds drifting over the ocean far below, looking like scattered snow on ice. The meaning comes clear as I write, an assurance from God that he holds John and me in his big hand and all he asks is our willing obedience. So I'm learning a familiar spiritual lesson all over again, at a profound level. I can feel the personal growth happening and the knowledge that God is culturing it, and me. What confidence this gives!

My journal was given back, and with it a sense of peace about the future and John. And I am filled with exhilaration.

Now, a year after that airport incident, John and I are married. God gave me back not only my journal, but with it an assurance that our friendship was full of promise, which he is now fulfilling. I am still keeping a journal, anticipating fresh understandings, new lessons learned from this new life.

For Further Reading

Elliot, Jim. *The Journals of Jim Elliot*, ed. Elisabeth Elliot. Old Tappan, N.J. Revell, 1978.

England, Edward (Editor). *Keeping a Spiritual Journal.* Crowborough, Highland Books, 1988.

Goldberg, Natalie. *Writing Down the Bones.* Boston: Shambhala, 1986.

Hagan, Kay Leigh. *Internal Affairs,* San Francisco: Harper & Row, 1990, 1988.

Klug, Ronald. *How to Keep a Spiritual Journal.* New York: Thomas Nelson, 1982.

Nouwen, Henri. *The Genesee Diary.* New York: Doubleday, 1976.

O'Connor, Elizabeth. *Search for Silence.* Waco: Word, 1972.

Progoff, Ira. *At a Journal Workshop.* New York: Dialogue House Library, 1975.

Sarton, May. *Journal of a Solitude.* New York: Norton, 1973.

Wakefield, Dan. *The Story of Your Life.* Boston: Beacon Press, 1990.

Zinsser, William (Ed.). *Inventing the Truth: The Art and Craft of Memoir.* Boston: Houghton Mifflin, 1987.

FOCUS

ON COLLEGE SUCCESS

Third Edition

Constance Staley
University of Colorado, Colorado Springs

WADSWORTH
CENGAGE Learning

Australia • Brazil • Japan • Korea • Mexico • Singapore • Spain • United Kingdom • United States

FOCUS on College Success, Third Edition
Constance Staley

Executive Editor: Shani Fisher

Senior Development Editor: Julia Giannotti

Assistant Editor: Joanna Hassel

Editorial Assistant: Sarah Turner

Media Editor: Amy Gibbons

Marketing Coordinator: Brittany Blais

Marketing Communications Manager:
Linda Yip

Content Project Manager: Jessica Rasile

Senior Art Director: Pamela Galbreath

Manufacturing Planner: Sandee Milewski

Rights Acquisition Specialist:
Shalice Shah-Caldwell

Production Service/Compositor:
MPS Limited, a Macmillan Company

Cover and Text Designer: Lisa Delgado

Cover Images: Larry Harwood Photography

For product information and technology assistance, contact us at
Cengage Learning Customer & Sales Support, 1-800-354-9706

For permission to use material from this text or product,
submit all requests online at **www.cengage.com/permissions**.
Further permissions questions can be emailed to
permissionrequest@cengage.com.

Library of Congress Control Number: 2011937591

ISBN-13: 978-1-111-82752-6

ISBN-10: 1-111-82752-4

Wadsworth
20 Channel Center Street
Boston, MA 02210
USA

Cengage Learning is a leading provider of customized learning solutions with office locations around the globe, including Singapore, the United Kingdom, Australia, Mexico, Brazil and Japan. Locate your local office at **international.cengage.com/region**

Cengage Learning products are represented in Canada by Nelson Education, Ltd.

For your course and learning solutions, visit **www.cengage.com**.

Purchase any of our products at your local college store or at our preferred online store **www.cengagebrain.com**.

Instructors: Please visit **login.cengage.com** and log in to access instructor-specific resources.

Printed in the United States of America
1 2 3 4 5 6 7 15 14 13 12 11